검정고시 입시 고수들의
만점 전략 수험서

최신 개정판

검고수 영어

만점전략서

고등학교 졸업자격 검정고시

한양학원 수험서 — 편집부 저

도서출판 국자감
www.kukjagam.co.kr

CONTENTS

검정고시 만점 전략

1. 개정 교육과정에 따른 고졸 영어의 출제 경향

어휘 5문항, 어법 1문항, 생활영어 7문항, 독해 12문항

① 독해 문항의 출제범위가 넓어지고 문제의 난이도가 올라감

② 문법(어법)보다는 읽고 이해(독해)하는 능력 평가에 치중함

③ 다양한 실용문(도표, 게시문, 그래프)이 출제됨

④ 어휘 문제는 의미가 같은 표현 찾기를 넘어서 다양한 형식으로 출제됨

2. 개정 교육과정에 따른 고졸 영어 학습 방법

① 단공신 등을 통한 지속적인 어휘학습이 필요함

② 독해 지문을 통한 유형별 문제 풀이 학습이 요구됨

③ 평소에 다양한 구문을 접하여 문장을 의미의 덩어리로 보는 연습이 필요함

④ 문법(어법)은 개념파악과 문장 내의 활용에 중점을 두어 학습해야 함

01. 어법

01 어법

1 명사와 대명사

[핵심 01] 명사 : 사람, 동식물, 사물의 이름을 나타내는 말

구분	셀 수 있는 명사	셀 수 없는 명사
단수명사	앞에 a(n)을 쓴다.	셀 수 없는 명사는 단수 및 복수 개념이 없다. 앞에 a(n)을 쓰지 않고 뒤에 -(e)s를 쓰지도 않는다.
복수명사	뒤에 -(e)s를 쓴다.	
종류	보통명사 : a book - books 집합명사 : family, police audience, cattle	물질명사 : coffee, salt, water 추상명사 : peace, advice, love 고유명사 : Seoul, the Pacific

· He has a good <u>computer</u>.

· There are many <u>computers</u> on the desk.

· They gave me some <u>milk</u>.

· We have much <u>experience</u>.

[핵심 02] 셀 수 없는 명사의 수량표시

> 셀 수 없는 명사(예 paper, coffee 등)는 단수 및 복수 개념이 없으므로 수를 표현하기 위해서는 셀 수 있는 명사(예 piece, cup 등)를 사용한다.

(1) 우유 한 잔 : a cup of milk
    우유 두 잔 : <u>two cups</u> of milk (O) / two cups of milks (X)

(2) 단위명사의 종류

명사 종류	단위명사	예시
water, juice, tea 등	glass, cup, bottle	two bottles of water
information, advice 등	piece	a piece of advice
bread, meat, soap 등	loaf	four loaves of bread

· I drink a cup of coffee after dinner.

· I heard a piece of interesting information.

대명사 : 명사의 반복을 피하기 위해 명사 대신 쓰는 말

대명사의 종류		의미	예시
인칭대명사	재귀대명사	'~자신' : -self , -selves	myself, himself, themselves …
	소유대명사	'~의 것'	mine, hers, ours …
지시대명사		앞, 뒤 어구를 가리킴	this (these), that (those)
부정대명사		불특정한 대상을 가리킴	one, all, some, both, either …

[핵심 03] 지시대명사

구분	단수	복수
가까운 곳의 사람, 사물 / 후자	this	these
먼 곳에 있는 사람, 사물 / 전자	that	those

· **This** is my brother.

· Could I have one of **these**?

· I have a dog and a cat; **that** is lovelier than **this**.

· The price of gold is much higher than **that** of silver.

[핵심 04] 부정대명사 one : 막연한 물건이나 일반인을 나타내는 대명사

· One should do one's best. (불특정 일반인)
· If you need a pen, here is one. (동일한 종류의 다른 것)

[핵심 05] 부정대명사의 표현방법

· I have two pens. One is a green, and the other is a red.
· I have three brothers. One is a doctor, another is a lawyer and the other is a teacher.
· I have four kids. One is in Seoul, and the others are in Busan.
· I have many books. Some are comic books, and others are novels.

1. 다음 우리말과 의미가 같도록 빈칸에 들어갈 말은?

> 나는 인형을 하나 가지고 있다.
> → I have ________ doll.

① an　② the　③ our　④ a

2. 다음 문장의 빈칸에 들어갈 알맞은 말은?

> I'd like to have a ________ of tea.

① pair　② cup　③ loaf　④ piece

3. 다음 문장의 빈칸에 들어갈 알맞은 말은?

> He is wearing a ____________.

① blue shirt　② glasses　③ earrings　④ pants

4. 주어진 우리말을 영어로 바르게 옮긴 것은?

> 그녀는 나에게 두 조각의 케이크를 주었다.

① She gave me cakes.
② She gave me two cakes.
③ She gave me a piece of cake.
④ She gave me two pieces of cake.

5. 다음 밑줄 친 부분에 들어갈 알맞은 말을 고르시오.

> ⓐ bottle　ⓑ paper　ⓒ table tennis　ⓓ piano　ⓔ shoes

1) I need three sheets of ____________.

2) Let's play ____________ after school.

3) He gave me a pair of ____________.

4) Please give me a ____________ of water.

※ [6~10] 다음 문장의 빈칸에 들어갈 알맞은 말은?

6.

Sumi, ________ is my sister, Hyejin.

① it ② this ③ those ④ they

7.

This hat is too old. I want a new ________.

① one ② ones ③ it ④ they

8.

Amy doesn't like cold drinks. She likes hot ________.

① one ② ones ③ any ④ some

9.

Some people like playing baseball; ________ do not.

① one ② others ③ another ④ the other

10.

There are two books. One is a novel, ________ is a comic book.

① one ② others ③ another ④ the other

2 형용사와 부사

형용사 : 명사 수식, 보어 역할 (주격보어와 목적격보어)
부사 : 형용사, 동사, 부사, 문장 전체를 수식 (장소, 방법, 시간 등)

명사 + ly ⇒ 형용사 : lovely, friendly, weekly …
형용사 + ly ⇒ 부사 : sadly, slowly, happily …

[핵심 06] 형용사가 명사보다 뒤에 오는 경우

원칙	형용사 + (대)명사 + to부정사	
예외	(대)명사 + 형용사 + to부정사	명사가 -thing, -body, -one으로 끝나는 경우

· She is a <u>beautiful girl</u>.
· There are many <u>interesting books to read</u> in the library.
· I saw <u>somebody strange</u> on my way home.
· Please, give me <u>something hot to drink</u>.

[핵심 07] 부정수량 형용사

명사	부정수량 형용사				
	많은	약간의	거의 없는	전혀 없는	많은
수 (셀 수 있는 명사)	many	a few	few	no	a lot of = lots of = plenty of
양 (셀 수 없는 명사)	much	a little	little		

· How <u>many</u> tickets do we need?

· I have <u>much</u> money in my pocket.

· We have <u>a few</u> eggs. Let's make an omelette.

· I have <u>a little</u> time to see him.

· I have <u>few</u> friends in my class.

· I have <u>little</u> interest in politics.

· I have <u>no</u> friend to go with there.

· I have <u>no</u> time to play computer games.

· There are <u>plenty of</u> ways for kids to help other kids.

· Don't hurry. There's <u>plenty of</u> time.

[핵심 8] 형용사+ly=부사 중 의미가 완전히 달라지는 부사

형용사와 부사		부사	
late	늦은 / 늦게	lately	최근에 = recently
near	가까운 / 가깝게	nearly	거의 = almost
high	높은 / 높게	highly	매우 = very
hard	어려운, 단단한 / 열심히	hardly	거의 ~하지 않다

· **Lately**, I met the doctor in the street.

· It took me **nearly** a week to finish the report.

· That was a **highly** successful play.

· He can **hardly** understand what I said.

[핵심 9] 형용사 및 부사의 변화

형용사와 부사가 성질, 상태, 수량 등의 정도를 비교하기 위해 어형변화를 하는데,
이를 비교라 하며, 「원급, 비교급, 최상급」으로 표현한다.

<table>
<tr><th>원급</th><th>비교급</th><th>최상급</th></tr>
<tr><td rowspan="4">원래 단어 형태 그대로</td><td>원급 + (e)r</td><td>원급 + (e)st</td></tr>
<tr><td>단어가 3음절 미만인 경우</td><td>단어가 3음절 미만인 경우</td></tr>
<tr><td>more + 원급</td><td>most + 원급</td></tr>
<tr><td>단어가 3음절 이상인 경우</td><td>단어가 3음절 이상인 경우</td></tr>
</table>

원급	비교급	최상급
fast	faster	fastest
famous	more famous	most famous
good / well	better	best
bad / ill	worse	worst
little	less	least
many / much	more	most

[핵심 10] 원급, 비교급, 최상급의 기본구조

원급 표현	**as 원급 ~ as …**	… 만큼 ~한/하게
비교 표현	**비교급 ~ than …**	… 보다 더 ~한/하게
최상급 표현	**the 최상급 ~ in 장소…/ of …**	…에서/…중에서 가장 ~한/하게

· He is **as tall as** Mike.

· He is not **as/so tall as** Mike.

· She is **older than** Su-mi.

· Sally is **more beautiful than** Jane.

· Tom is **the tallest** boy in his class.

· Time is **the most precious** thing of all.

[핵심 11] 비교급의 다양한 표현들

구분	표현	해석
1	**get + 비교급 and 비교급**	점점 더 ~하게 되다.
	It's getting **darker and darker.**	
2	**The + 비교급 ~, the + 비교급 …**	~하면 할수록 점점 더 …하게 되다.
	The more you eat, **the fatter** you become.	
3	**The + 비교급 of the two**	둘 중에 더 ~하다.
	He is **the taller of the two** boys.	

[핵심 12] 최상급을 나타내는 여러 가지 표현

구분	최상급 표현
1	the + 최상급
2	비교급 + than any other + 단수명사
3	부정주어 + 비교급 + than
4	부정주어 + as/so + 원급 + as

· He is **the tallest student** in his class.

· He is **taller than any other student** in his class.

· **No student** is **taller than** he in his class.

· **No student** is **as tall as** he in his class.

· Time is **the most precious thing** of all.

· Time is **more precious than any other thing.**

· Time is **more precious than anything else.**

· **Nothing** is **more precious than** time.

· **Nothing** is **so precious as** time.

※ [1~2] 다음 빈칸에 알맞지 않은 것을 고르시오.

1. How many ________ do you have?

① books ② oranges ③ money ④ shirts

2. Are there ________ students in the classroom?

① many ② much ③ a lot of ④ some

3. 다음 밑줄 친 부분 중 어법상 어색한 것은?

① There are so much flowers.
② We have much snow in winter.
③ I have many old friends.
④ We can do many things.

4. 다음 밑줄 친 부분 중 어법상 어색한 것은?

① Miso was eating a late breakfast.
② She plays the piano well.
③ I have an interesting book.
④ The worker worked hardly.

※ [5~6] John의 가족에 관한 표를 보고 다음 대화의 빈칸에 알맞은 말을 고르시오.

	나이	키	몸무게
Kim	43	170cm	65kg
Bettie	40	160cm	52kg
John	14	172cm	60kg
Ann	12	150cm	40kg

5.

A : Who's the ________ in the family?
B : Ann.

① oldest ② youngest ③ tallest ④ heaviest

6.

A : Who's the tallest person in the family?
B : ___________.

① Kim ② Bettie ③ John ④ Ann

7. 다음 두 단어의 관계가 나머지 셋과 다른 하나는?

① tall – taller
② early – earlier
③ late – later
④ swim – swimmer

※ [8~9] 다음 빈칸에 알맞은 것을 고르시오.

8.

They have the ________ seafood in town.

① good ② gooder ③ better ④ best

9.

Kim is 18 years old and Choi is 20 years old. Kim is __________ than Choi.

① more young
② younger
③ the youngest
④ more young

10. 다음 괄호 안에 주어진 단어의 형태를 바르게 고친 것은?

· Mary is (fast) than Ann.
· Tommy is the (fast) runner of all.
· This plane can fly three times as (fast) as that one.

① fast – fast – fast
② fast – faster – faster
③ fastest – fast – faster
④ faster – fastest – fast

3 문장의 형식

[핵심 13] 문장의 구성

형식	문장의 구성 요소	해석 방법
1형식	S + V (주어 + 완전자동사) The sun disappeared.	S가 V하다 태양이 사라졌다.
2형식	S + V + S.C (주어 + 불완전자동사 + 주격보어) He is my son. She became a doctor.	S는 SC이다 / S는 SC가 되다 그는 나의 아들이다. 그녀는 의사가 되었다.
3형식	S + V + O (주어 + 완전타동사 + 목적어) I need you.	S는 O를 V하다 나는 당신이 필요해요.
4형식	S + V + I.O + D.O (주어 + 완전타동사 + 간접목적어 + 직접목적어) I gave you my heart.	S는 IO에게 DO를 V하다 나는 너에게 마음을 주었다.
5형식	S + V + O + O.C (주어 + 불완전타동사 + 목적어 + 목적격보어) They call me a poet. He made me angry.	S가 O를 OC라고 V하다 S는 O가 OC 하는 것을 V하다 그들은 나를 시인이라 부른다. 그가 나를 화나게 만들었다.

주격보어 or 목적격보어 자리에는

명사, 형용사, to 부정사, 분사 등이 온다.

· My sister is <u>a high school student</u>.

· The sofa looks <u>comfortable</u>.

· I asked him <u>to call</u> her first.

· Don't leave the baby <u>crying</u>.

[핵심 14] 지각동사, 사역동사

(1) 사역동사 + 목적어 + 동사원형

make, have, let / help(준사역동사)

· My friend **made** me **wait** too long.

· We won't **let** you **eat** too many sweets.

· I **helped** her **(to) move** the table.

→ help는 목적격보어 자리에 동사원형, to부정사 모두 가능

(2) 지각(=감각)동사 + 목적어 + 동사원형(현재분사)

see, watch, look at, hear, listen to, taste, feel 등

· Did you **hear** Paul sing that song?

· I **saw** her smile brightly.

· **Look at** the clown jumping high.

· I **felt** the building shaking.

→ 현재분사 형태는 동작의 '진행'의 의미를 강조

※ [1~2] 다음 빈칸에 알맞지 않은 것을 고르시오.

1. Jay looks ________ today.

① tired ② happily ③ sad ④ down

2. My friend ________ me a book.

① gave ② bought ③ passed ④ said

3. 다음 문장을 영어로 바르게 옮긴 것을 고르면?

한 선생님께서 우리에게 수학을 가르치신다.

① Mr. Han teaches math with us.
② Mr. Han teaches to us math.
③ Mr. Han teach math for us.
④ Mr. Han teaches us math.

4. 다음 빈칸에 들어갈 전치사가 나머지 셋과 다른 것은?

① My mom made a cake ______ me.
② He told a ghost story ______ me.
③ I wrote a letter ______ my teacher.
④ Mark sent a birthday card ______ me.

5. 다음 중 어법상 어색한 것은?

① That sounds wonderful.
② This food tastes badly.
③ She feels really sick.
④ You look very good.

6. 다음 우리말과 뜻이 같아지도록 할 때 괄호 안 동사의 형태로 알맞은 것은?

> Jenny는 우리가 그 의자를 옮기기를 원했다.
> → Jenny wanted us (move) the chair.

① move ② moved ③ to move ④ moving

7. 다음 빈칸에 들어갈 말이 바르게 짝지어진 것은?

> · Kim wrote a letter ______ her friend.
> · I will buy a hat ______ my sister.

① to − for ② for − for ③ to − of ④ of − to

8. 다음 대화의 빈칸에 알맞은 것은?

> A : You look ________. What's up?
> B : I didn't pass my math test.

① sadly ② sad ③ sadness ④ being sad

9. 다음 밑줄 친 단어의 의미가 나머지 셋과 <u>다른</u> 것은?

① I <u>made</u> my friend angry.
② She <u>makes</u> me sad.
③ They <u>make</u> the air clean.
④ My brother <u>made</u> me a box.

10. 다음 글의 밑줄 친 ⓐ ~ ⓓ 중 어법상 <u>어색한</u> 것은?

> She ⓐ <u>looked</u> ⓑ <u>down</u> yesterday. I asked her ⓒ <u>explaining</u> the situation. Finally, she told ⓓ <u>me</u> about the accident.

4 동사 시제

시제 : 동작과 상태가 언제 일어나느냐를 나타내는 동사의 형태 변화

[핵심 15] 시간과 조건의 부사절에서 현재가 미래를 대신한다.

단어	의미	미래시제 가능 여부
when	언제 (명사절)	+ will 가능
	~할 때 (미래의미 포함) - 부사절	+ will 불가
if	~인지 아닌지 (명사절)	+ will 가능
	만약 ~라면 (미래의미 포함) - 부사절	+ will 불가

· I don't know <u>when he **will come** home</u>. (명사절)

· <u>When he **comes** home</u>, I will have a party. (부사절)

· I don't know <u>if it **will rain** tomorrow</u>. (명사절)

· <u>If it **rains** tomorrow</u>, I won't go out. (부사절)

[핵심 16] 현재완료시제의 이해

현재완료 : 현재의 한 시점을 기준으로 과거의 어느 때부터 현재까지의 동작의 완료(막 ~다했다), 경험(~한 적이 있다), 결과(지금도 그 결과가 계속되고 있다), 상태의 계속(쭉 계속해왔다) 등을 나타낸다.

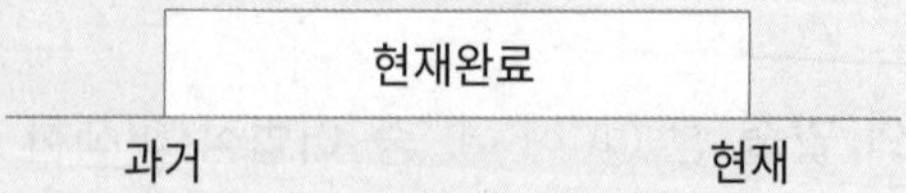

•I lost my book. (과거)

•I have lost my book. (현재완료)

= I lost my book so I don't have it now.

종류	의미	특징
have(has) been to ★	★에 가본 적이 있다.	현재 ★에 없다.
have(has) gone to ★	★에 가버리고 없다.	현재 ★에 있다.

· Min-ho went to America last year and he is in Seoul now.

⇒ Min-ho <u>**has been to**</u> America.

· Min-ho went to America last year and he is in America now.

⇒ Min-ho <u>**has gone to**</u> America.

[핵심 17] 과거완료시제의 이해

과거완료 : 과거보다 한 시제 이전에 일어난 사건을 표현할 때 주로 사용하며 과거시제와 항상 함께 쓰이는 것이 원칙이다.

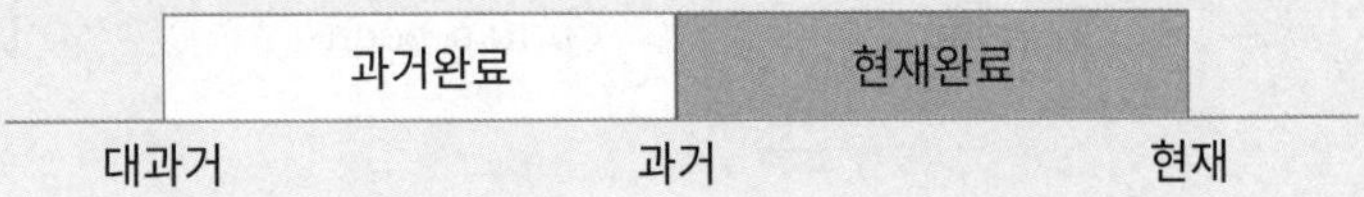

· When the police **caught** the thief, he **had spent** all the money.

· When I **arrived** at the airport, the plane **had taken** off.

※ [1~4] 다음 빈칸에 알맞은 것을 고르시오.

1. Seoul ______ the capital city of Korea.

① be ② will ③ was ④ is

2. Lily ________ go to the concert tomorrow.

① be ② will ③ was ④ is

3. Jane _______ a movie last night.

① watch ② will watch ③ watched ④ is watching

4. Carol ________ to Canada twice.

① was ② went ③ has been ④ had gone

5. 다음 문장을 영어로 바르게 옮긴 것을 고르면?

너는 3년 동안 계속 영어를 공부해 오고 있니?

① Has you studying English for 3 years?
② Have you studying English since 3 years?
③ Have you studied English for 3 years?
④ Has you been studying English since 3 years?

6. 어법상 대화의 빈칸에 알맞은 말은?

A : Was your sister playing the piano last night?
B : ____________________

① Yes, she is.
② Yes, she was.
③ Yes, she did.
④ No, she isn't.

※ [7~10] 다음 문장의 빈칸에 들어갈 말로 알맞은 것을 고르시오.

7. The earth ____________ around the sun.

① move
② moved
③ moves
④ had moved

8. I will have lunch when she ____________ home.

① return
② returns
③ will return
④ returned

9. We will go on a picnic if it ___________ tomorrow.

① will not
② is not rain
③ does not rain
④ has not rained

10. He told me that Columbus ___________ America in 1542.

① discovers
② discovered
③ had discovered
④ has discovered

5 조동사

> 조동사 : 동사의 한 종류. 동사와 함께 쓰여, 그 동사를 도와주는 역할을 한다.
> 조동사와 함께 쓰이는 동사를 본동사라 하며 반드시 동사원형을 쓴다.

[핵심 18] 조동사 must와 should

구분	표현	의미
1	must	~해야 한다 (= have to) ↔ don't have to ~할 필요 없다
2	must be	~임이 틀림없다. ↔ can't be ~일리가 없다
3	must not	~해서는 안 된다. (강한 금지)
4	must have p.p	~이었음이 틀림없다. (과거 사실에 대한 단정)
5	should	~해야 한다 (= ought to)
6	should have p.p	~했어야만 했는데 (과거 사실에 대한 비난 / 후회)

· You **must** study very hard to pass the exam.

· You **must not** smoke here.

· He **must be** rich now.

= It is **certain** that he **is** rich now.

· He **must have been** rich those days.

= It is **certain** that he **was** rich those days.

· I think he **should** brush his teeth three times a day.

· She **should have done** the work.

· I **shouldn't have bought** the cap.

[핵심 19] 조동사 can / could

구분	표현	의미
1	가능 / 능력	~할 수 있다 (= be able to)
2	허락	~해도 좋다 (= may)
3	can't have p.p	~이었을 리가 없다
4	관용표현	can't help ~ing ~하지 않을 수 없다 can't ~ too much 아무리 ~해도 지나치지 않다

· He **can** play the guitar.
  = He **is able to** play the guitar.
· You **can** use my cellphone.
· She **can't have gone** there last night.
  = It is **impossible** that she **went** there last night.
· I **can't help doing** my best.
· I **can't** thank you **too much.**

[핵심 20] 조동사 used to와 관련된 중요 구문

구분	내용	의미
1	used	use(사용하다)의 과거(분사)형
2	used to + 동사원형	~하곤 했다. (과거의 규칙적인 습관, 현재X)
3	be used to + 동사원형ing	~하는 데 익숙하다. (사람주어)
4	be used to + 동사원형	~하는 데 사용되다. (사물주어)

· I **used** the tool to fix the machine.

· He bought a **used** car.

· I **used to go** to school by bus.

· I **am used to doing** such a thing.

· The tool **is used to fix** the machine.

[핵심 21] had better / would rather

구분	내용	의미
1	had better + 동사원형	~ 하는 게 더 낫다 (충고, 가벼운 명령) ↔ had better not + 동사원형
2	would rather + 동사원형	(…하기보다는) 차라리 ~하겠다 (선호)

· You **had better** go there right now.

= **Why don't you** go there right now?

· You'**d better not** go there right now.

· I'**d rather** go skiing tomorrow than today.

· I **would rather** not tell you.

1. 두 문장의 뜻을 같게 할 때, 다음 빈칸에 들어갈 말로 알맞은 것을 고르시오.

> Is a penguin able to fly? → ________ a penguin fly?

① Can ② May ③ Should ④ Must

2. 다음 밑줄 친 부분과 뜻이 가까운 것은?

> Hello. Can I speak to Mike?

① May I talk to Insu? ② Books should be returned on time.
③ Henry can speak Spanish. ④ That rumor cannot be true.

3. 다음 빈칸에 들어갈 말 중, 나머지와 의미가 전혀 다른 하나는?

> A : Haven't you watched the movie, The Truman Show?
> B : Not yet.
> A : Then you _____ watch it!

① have to ② should ③ must ④ may

※ [4~6] 우리말과 뜻을 같게 할 때, 빈칸에 알맞은 말을 〈보기〉에서 고르시오.

〈보기〉

① may ② must ③ can't ④ should ⑤ shouldn't

4. 그는 늦잠 잤음에 틀림없다.
→ He ________ have overslept.

5. 그녀는 몸무게를 더 줄이지 말았어야 했다.
→ She ________ have lost more weight.

6. 그 가게는 벌써 닫았을지도 모른다.
→ The store ________ have closed already.

※ [7~8] 우리말과 뜻을 같게 할 때, 빈칸에 알맞은 말을 고르시오.

7. 어린 시절에 그와 나는 야구를 하곤 했다.
→ He and I _______ play baseball in our childhood

① would ② used to ③ would rather ④ need to

8. 나는 복권을 사느니 차라리 저축을 하겠다.
→ I _________ save money than buy Lottery.

① would ② used to ③ would rather ④ had rather

9. 다음 대화의 밑줄 친 부분과 뜻이 가까운 것은?

Some students don't need to wear school uniforms.
→ Some students _______ wear school uniforms.

① must not ② should not
③ has not to ④ don't have to

10. 대화에서 밑줄 친 부분의 의도로 가장 알맞은 것은?

A : Why are you so late?
B : I was stuck in traffic. I <u>shouldn't have driven</u>.

① 의심 ② 후회 ③ 동의 ④ 제안

6 준동사

준동사 : 한 문장에는 하나의 동사만 오는 것이 원칙이다. 그 이외의 동사는 동사의 기능을 간직하면서 다른 품사(명사, 형용사, 부사)의 기능을 하게 되는데, 이를 준동사라 한다. 준동사에는 부정사, 동명사, 분사가 있다.

[핵심 22] to부정사 (to+동사원형)

· 부정사 : 「to + 동사원형」의 형태

· 명사적 용법 : 문장 안에서 주어, 목적어, 보어 역할
· 형용사적 용법 : 명사를 수식
· 부사적 용법 : 목적, 결과, 감정의 원인, 판단의 근거 등

1. 명사적 용법
   · **To tell** a lie is wrong. [주어]
   = It is wrong **to tell** a lie. [가주어, 진주어]
   · His hobby is **to play** mobile games. [주격보어]
   · She wants **to be** a doctor when she grows up. [목적어]
   · I think it dangerous **to travel** alone. [가목적어, 진목적어]

2. 형용사적 용법
   · He was the first man **to reach** the North Pole.
   · She bought an interesting book **to read**.
   · We are looking for an apartment **to live in**.

· We **are to meet** here at ten. [예정]

· You **are to obey** the traffic rules. [의무]

· If you **are to succeed**, you must do your best. [의도]

· Nothing **was to be seen** in the night sky. [가능]

· He **was** never **to see** his family. [운명]

3. 부사적 용법

· We eat **to live**, not live **to eat**. [목적]

· The girl grew up **to become** a famous musician. [결과]

· She was surprised **to hear** the news. [감정의 원인]

· He must be crazy **to do** such a thing. [판단의 근거]

[핵심 23] to부정사의 문장 전환

구 (단문)	절 (복문)
in order to Root …	so that - may …
…하기 위해서	
too ~ to Root …	so ~ that - can't …
너무 ~해서 …할 수 없다	
~ enough to Root …	so ~ that - can …
너무 ~해서 …할 수 있다	

· He studied hard **in order to pass** the exam.
= He studied hard **so that** he **might** pass the exam.

· She is **too** young **to go** to school.
= She is **so** young **that** she **can't go** to school.

· The box was **too** heavy for him **to carry**.
= The box was **so** heavy **that** he **couldn't carry** it.

· She was smart **enough to solve** the problem.
= She was **so** smart **that** she **could solve** the problem.

[핵심 24] 부정사의 의미상의 주어

가주어	형용사	의미상 주어	진주어
[일반] It is	이성적 판단 important, hard, difficult, easy 등	for + 목적격	to + 동사원형
[예외] It is	인간의 성질, 상태 kind, wise, clever, foolish 등	of + 목적격	to + 동사원형

· **It** is ***important*** for him **to study** English everyday.
· **It** is ***hard*** for me **to memorize** those words by tomorrow.
· **It** was ***foolish*** of her **to do** such a thing.
· **It** is ***kind*** of them **to help** the poor every weekend.

[핵심 25] 독립부정사

구분	구문	의미
1	to tell the truth	사실대로 말하자면
2	to begin with	우선, 무엇보다도
3	to make matters worse	설상가상으로, 엎친 데 덮친 격으로
4	strange to say	이상한 말이지만
5	needless to say	말할 필요도 없이, 두말할 나위도 없이

· **To tell the truth**, I love her very much.

· **To begin with**, you must study English.

· **To make matters worse**, it rained a lot.

· **Strange to say**, he must be mad.

· **Needless to say**, she must be a liar.

[핵심 26] 동명사와 to부정사

동명사 : 「동사원형 + ~ing」
동사와 명사의 기능을 겸하며 주어, 목적어, 보어 역할
'~하는 것, ~하기'로 해석

주어	동사	목적어(동사일 때)
명사 혹은 대명사	stop, finish, give up, avoid, mind, enjoy 등	동명사(동사원형 + ing)
	want, hope, expect, decide, promise, plan 등	to부정사(to + 동사원형)
	love, like, start, begin continue, hate 등	동명사 혹은 to부정사 (둘 다 가능하고 의미 차이 없음)
	remember, forget	to부정사 (미래) (~해야 할 것을 기억한다/잊다) 동명사 (과거) (~했던 것을 기억한다/잊다)

· He **finished** ***doing*** his homework last night.

· Mike **wants** ***to become*** a doctor in the future.

· He **likes to** ***watch***(= ***watching***) TV.

· I **remember** ***to meet*** her in the office tomorrow morning.

· I **remember** ***meeting*** her in the office last month.

[핵심 27] 동명사의 관용적 표현

구분	표현	의미
1	cannot help ~ing	~하지 않을 수 없다
	I cannot help doing my homework now. = I can't but do my homework now.	
2	It is no use ~ing	~해도 소용이 없다
	It is no use crying over the spilt milk. = It is useless to cry over the spilt milk.	
3	There is no ~ing	~하는 것은 불가능하다
	There is no finishing the work within a week. = It is impossible to finish the work within a week.	
4	cannot(=never) … without ~ing	…할 때마다 반드시 ~하다
	They can't meet without fighting. = Whenever they meet, they always fight.	
5	feel like ~ing	~하고 싶은 생각이 들다
	I feel like reading the book today. = I feel inclined to read the book today.	
6	be busy (in) ~ing	~하느라 바쁘다
	They are busy (in) preparing for the examination.	
7	keep A from ~ing	A가 ~하는 것을 막다
	My mother kept me from going to the concert.	

구분	표현	의미
8	On(= Upon) ~ing	~하자마자
	On hearing the news, he was surprised. = As soon as he heard the news, he was surprised.	
9	It goes without saying that ~	~은 말할 것도 없다
	It goes without saying that honesty is the best policy. = It is needless to say that honesty is the best policy.	
10	be used to ~ing	~하는 데 익숙하다
	Janet is used to cooking Korean food.	
11	look forward to ~ing	~을 고대하다
	He looks forward to meeting her again.	
12	spend + 돈, 시간 + (on/in) + ~ing	~하는 데 돈, 시간 등을 소비하다
	I spent much money buying the new car. I spend two hours watching television everyday.	
13	have difficulty/trouble + (in) + ~ing	~하는 데 어려움을 겪다
	We have difficulty (in) finding the house. I always have trouble waking up in the morning.	

[핵심 28] 분사의 용법

분사 : 동사적인 성격과 형용사적인 성격을 가진다.

현재분사(동사원형 + ~ing) : 능동과 진행의 의미

과거분사(p.p) : 수동과 완료의 의미

* 분사를 이용하여 특별한 형태의 구문(분사구문)을 만들기도 한다.

구분	종류	예문
한정적 용법 - 명사 수식	현재분사 : 동사원형 + ing → 능동, 진행의 의미	I saw the **crying** girl right here.
		Do you know the man **standing** at the gate?
	과거분사 : p.p → 수동, 완료의 의미	Look at the **fallen** leaves.
		Yesterday I got a letter **written** in English.
서술적 용법 - 보어 역할	주격보어 : 주어를 보충설명	I feel **tired** all the time.
		He stood **watching** TV.
	목적보어 : 목적어를 보충설명	I heard him **playing** the guitar.
		Leave the door **closed**.

[핵심 29] 분사구문

- 시간, 이유, 조건, 양보 등의 부사절과 부대상황(연속동작, 동시동작)의 종속절을 분사를 이용하여 간단히 만든 형태의 문장이다.

분사구문 만드는 법

① 부사절(종속절)의 접속사를 생략한다.
② 부사절(종속절)의 주어와 주절의 주어가 같으면 생략하고, 다르면 그대로 둔다.
③ 부사절(종속절)과 주절의 시제가 같으면 부사절의 동사를 「동사원형 + ~ing」 형태로, 한 시제 앞서면 「having + p.p」의 형태로 쓴다.
④ 부사절(종속절)의 동사가 수동태이면
동사를 「being + p.p」로, 한 시제 앞서면 「having been + p.p」로 나타낸다.
* 이때 being이나 having been은 생략할 수 있다.

(능동) Because she had a fever, she couldn't go shopping.

= Having a fever, she couldn't go shopping.

(완료) As he had done it before, he knew how to do it.

= Having done it before, he knew how to do it.

(수동) When he is compared with other boys, he is sensible.

= (Being) Compared with other boys, he is sensible.

(완료형 수동) As I have been raised in France, I speak French well.

= (Having been) Raised in France, I speak French well.

구분	의미	예문
1	시간 when, as, while, after	When she heard the news, she began to cry. = **Hearing the news**, she began to cry.
2	원인, 이유 because, as	Because he was sick, he was absent from school. = **Being sick**, he was absent from school.
3	조건 if	If you turn to the right there, you will find the building. = **Turning to the right there**, you will find the building.
4	양보 though, although	Though I live next to his house, I don't know him. = **Living next to his house**, I don't know him.
5	연속동작 and	The train leaves at six, and it arrives in Seoul at noon. = The train leaves at six, **arriving in Seoul at noon**.
6	동시동작 as	He went out of the house as he said "Good-bye". = **Saying "Good-bye"**, he went out of the house.

[핵심 30] 독립분사구문

분사구문을 만들 때, 부사절의 주어와 주절의 주어가 다른 경우에, 부사절의 주어를 남겨 두는데, 이를 '**독립분사구문**'이라 한다.

If it is fine tomorrow, I will go on a picnic.
= **It being fine tomorrow**, I will go on a picnic.

As the bookstore was closed, I could not buy our textbook.
= **The bookstore being closed**, I could not buy our textbook.

단, 주절과 부사절의 주어가 다르더라도, 부사절 주어가 we, you, they, people 등과 같은 일반인일 때 주어를 생략하는데 이를 '**비인칭 독립분사구문**' 이라 한다.

구분	표현	의미
1	Judging from his accent, he must be a foreigner.	~로 판단해 볼 때
2	Generally speaking, women live longer than men.	일반적으로 말하자면
3	Strictly speaking, what he said is false.	엄밀하게 말하자면
4	Considering his age, he looks so young.	~을 고려해 볼 때
5	Roughly speaking, he spent two hours watching TV everyday.	대략적으로 말해서

단원확인문제

※ [1~7] 다음 문장의 빈칸에 들어갈 말로 알맞은 것을 고르시오.

1. __________ the street without looking both ways is dangerous.

① Cross ② Be crossing ③ Crossed ④ Crossing

2. You're big enough _______ the bike.

① ride ② rode ③ to ride ④ rides

3. His arms were too short _______ the shelf.

① to reach ② reach ③ reaching ④ be reached

4. He's good at ________ English.

① speak ② speaking ③ to speak ④ speaks

5. I can't help _______ when he talks about funny story.

① laugh ② to laughing ③ laughing ④ to laugh

6. My friend has difficulty _______ the twins apart. * tell : 구분하다

① telling ② to tell ③ tells ④ told

7.

Reading the book is so _______ to me.

① bore ② bored ③ boring ④ to bore

8. 다음 문장의 빈칸에 공통으로 들어갈 말로 알맞은 것을 고르시오.

· It is kind _______ her to help the poor.
· The cup is full _______ water.

① for ② with ③ of ④ from

9. 다음 대화의 밑줄 친 부분과 의미가 가까운 것은?

<u>As I watch</u> the news every day, I know what's going on in the world.

① Watching ② Watched
③ To watching ④ To be watched

10. 다음 대화의 밑줄 친 부분과 의미가 가까운 것은?

<u>Because she is a vegetarian</u>, Mary doesn't eat meat.

* vegetarian : 채식주의자

① Be a vegetarian ② Being a vegetarian
③ Because is a vegetarian ④ Mary be a vegetarian

7 수동태

주어와 동사의 능동 · 수동 관계를 나타내는 문장의 형식을 태라 한다.

능동태 : 「주어가 ~을 …하다」 같이 주어가 동작을 행하는 형태

수동태 : 「주어가 ~에 의해 …당하다」 같이 주어가 동작을 받거나 당하는 형태

▧ 수동태 만드는 법

① 능동태의 목적어를 주어로 한다. (a doll → A doll)

② 능동태의 동사를 「be동사 + 과거분사(p.p)」로 고친다.(makes → is made)

③ 능동태의 주어를「by + 목적격」의 형태로 바꾼다. (She → by her)

She makes a doll.

A doll is made by her.

진행형 수동태	be + being p.p
완료형 수동태	have(has, had) been + p.p

Somebody is cleaning the room at the moment.

→ The room **is being cleaned** at the moment.

We have postponed the concert because of the rain.

→ The concert **has been postponed** because of the rain.

[핵심 31] 수동태의 관용적 표현

구분	구문	의미
1	They were surprised at the news.	~에 놀라다
2	I was pleased with the gift.	~로 기뻐하다
3	We are satisfied with the result.	~에 만족하다
4	The doctor is known to everybody.	~에게 알려지다
5	I am tired with walking.	~에 피곤하다
6	I am tired of eggs.	~에 싫증나다
7	I am interested in English.	~에 흥미가 있다
8	The table was covered with books.	~로 덮여 있다
9	Butter is made from milk.	(화학적) ~로 만들어지다
10	The desk is made of wood.	(물리적) ~로 만들어지다

단원확인문제

※ [1~3] 다음 문장의 빈칸에 들어갈 말로 알맞은 것을 고르시오.

1.

An important meeting ______ in a conference room now.

① holds ② is held
③ is holding ④ is being held

2.

The new product ________ next week.

① launches ② will launch
③ will be launched ④ was launced

3.

A new bridge ________ in 1950.

① builds ② built
③ was building ④ was built

4. The singer is known (to, of, with) many young people.

5. Is she interested (in, with, of) dancing?

6. My mom is surprised (at, to, with) the noise.

7. His office is filled (of, with, by) books.

※ [8~10] 다음 빈칸에 들어갈 알맞은 말을 〈보기〉에서 고르시오.

〈보기〉

① with ② by ③ in ④ from ⑤ of

8. The shopping mall is crowded ________ people.

9. I have been interested ________ skiing since I was young.

10. Cheese is made ________ milk.

8 의문사와 관계사

의문사와 관계사는 형태는 같지만, 문장 속에서의 위치와 역할이 다르므로 그 쓰임에 따라 의문사, 접속사, 관계대명사, 관계부사로 구별한다.

의문사 / 접속사 / 관계사					
의문부사 / 관계부사			의문대명사 / 관계대명사		
시간	언제	when	사람	누가	who – whom - whose
장소	어디서	where	사물	무엇	what
방법	어떻게	how	선택	어느 것	which
이유	왜	why			

[핵심 32] 간접의문문 : 직접의문문이 다른 문장의 일부가 되어 명사절로 쓰임

의문문	직접의문문	의문사 + (조)동사 + 주어 ~?
	간접의문문	… 의문사 + 주어 + 동사 ~?

(1) 의문사가 있는 경우 : 의 + 주 + 동

· I don't know + Who is he?

⇒ I don't know <u>**who he is**</u>.

· Do you know + Where does she live?

⇒ Do you know <u>**where she lives**</u>?

(2) 의문사가 없는 경우 : **if(= whether) + 주 + 동**

· I don't know + Will it rain tomorrow?

⇒ I don't know **if(= whether) it will rain tomorrow**.

· Do you know + Is he happy?

⇒ Do you know **if(= whether) he is happy**?

(3) 주절이 의문문이고, 주절의 동사가 think, believe, guess, imagine, suppose 등이 오면 **의문사가 문장 앞**으로 나간다.

· Do you **know**? + How old is he?

⇒ Do you know **how old he is**?

· Do you **think**? + How old is he?

⇒ **How old** do you think **he is**?

[핵심 32] 관계대명사

- 접속사 + 대명사의 역할을 한다.

선행사	주격 관계대명사	소유격 관계대명사	목적격 관계대명사
사람	who	whose	who(m)
사물, 동물	which	whose, of which	which
사람, 사물, 동물	that	-	that
선행사 없음	what	-	what

- 앞 문장 전체를 받을 때는 무조건 which를 쓴다.
- 앞에 명사(선행사)가 없으면 무조건 what을 쓴다.

· This is the boy **who** likes to play tennis.
· This is the boy **whom** I want to meet.
· This is the boy **whose** name is Jack.

· The book **which** is on the table is mine.
· This is the book **which** I bought yesterday.
· Find the book **whose** cover is very old.

· She didn't say anything, **which** made him sad.

· We should do **what** is right.
· Show me **what** you bought.

[핵심 34] 관계부사

- 접속사 + 부사의 역할을 한다.

선행사	관계부사
장소 (the place)	where
시간 (the time)	when
이유 (the reason)	why
방법 (the way)	how

- the way와 how는 함께 쓸 수 없다.

· I went to the place **where** he lived last year.
· I remember the time **when** we met him for the first time.
· I don't know the reason **why** he didn't come home last night.
· I want to know **how** he studies English.

※ [1~3] 다음 (　　　) 안에서 알맞은 것을 고르시오.

1. I interviewed an actor (who, which) is very popular.

2. The rich man has a building (who, that) is located in the downtown.

3. That computer is (which, what) I want.

4. 다음 빈칸에 들어갈 알맞은 말을 고르시오.

Do you know the boy _______ can swim well?

① who　　② what　　③ whose　　④ which

※ [5~7] 다음 (　　　) 안에서 알맞은 것을 고르시오.

5. This is the place (where, when) we used to visit.

6. Sunday is the day (whose, when) she goes to church.

7. I told him (the way how, how) I made the wooden chair.

※ [8~10] 다음 빈칸에 들어갈 말로 알맞은 것을 고르시오.

8. The place _______ we met before is in front of the art gallery.

① who ② why ③ where ④ which

9. Do you remember the year _______ we had the Pyeongchang Olympic?

① when ② why ③ where ④ which

10. I don't know the reason _______ I got a poor grade.

① when ② why ③ where ④ which

9 가정법

[핵심 35] 가정법 기본공식

종류	문장 형식
가정법 과거 (현재 사실 반대)	If + 주어 + 동사의 과거형(were), 주어 + [조동사의 과거형 + 동사원형]
가정법 과거완료 (과거 사실 반대)	If + 주어 + had p.p~ , 주어 + [조동사의 과거형 + have p.p]
혼합 가정법 (현재까지 미치는 과거사실의 반대)	If + 주어 + had p.p~ , 주어 + [조동사의 과거형 + 동사원형]

· If I were a bird, I could fly to you.

· If I had much money, I could buy it to you.

· If he had given me a flower, I would have been happy.

· If I had taken her advice, I would have a fortune now.

[핵심 36] I wish 가정법 / as if 가정법

가정법	직설법
if	as (= because)
I wish 가정법 (~하면 좋을 텐데)	I am sorry (실현 불가능한 소망)
as if 가정법 (마치~인 것처럼)	in fact (실제와 다른 상황)

· If I were rich, I could buy the house. (가정법 과거)

⇒ As I am not rich, I can't buy the house. (직설법 현재)

· If he had studied hard, he would have passed the exam. (가정법 과거완료)

⇒ As he didn't study hard, he didn't pass the exam. (직설법 과거)

· **I wish** I were a doctor. (가정법 과거)

⇒ **I am sorry** I am not a doctor. (직설법 현재)

· He talks **as if** he knew the answer. (가정법 과거)

⇒ **In fact**, he doesn't know the answer. (직설법 현재)

※ [1~2] 다음 빈칸에 알맞은 것을 고르시오.

1. If I _______ tall, I could be more confident.

① was ② would be ③ were ④ am

2. If I _______ an architect, I would design my own house.

① was ② were ③ be ④ am

3. 다음 밑줄 친 부분을 어법에 맞게 고치시오.

It's cold outside. If I were you, I <u>will</u> put on a warm jacket.

※ [4~5] 우리말과 뜻이 같도록 주어진 말을 이용하여 문장을 완성하시오.

4. 네가 나를 도와주었다면, 나는 시험에 합격했을 텐데. (pass)

If you had helped me, I _______________ the exam.

5. 내가 그 책을 가지고 있었다면 너에게 빌려주었을 텐데. (have)

If I _______________ the book, I would have lent it to you.

6. 빈칸에 들어갈 말이 바르게 짝지어진 것은?

· If I _______ you, I would take a rest.
· If Mark had called, I _______ the ringing sound.

① was – would hear
② had been – would have heard
③ were – would hear
④ were – would have heard

※ [7~9] 다음 (   ) 안에서 알맞은 말을 고르시오.

7. I wish I (were, was) a millionaire now.

8. I wish I (can, could) have been more patient at that time.

9. He talks as if he (is, were) single, but he got married.

10. 두 문장의 뜻을 같게 할 때, 빈칸에 알맞은 것을 고르시오.

I'm sorry I can't participate in the school event.
→ I wish I _______ in the school event.

① participate
② could participate
③ couldn't participate
④ didn't participate

10 접속사와 전치사

접속사 + 주어 + 동사 - 문장과 문장을 연결하는 역할
전치사 + (대)명사/ 동명사 - 형용사구 혹은 부사구의 역할

· He went out for a walk **after** he had dinner.
⇒ He went out for a walk **after** dinner.
· **Because** it rained heavily, I couldn't go there in time.
⇒ **Because of** the heavy rain, I couldn't go there in time.
· **Though** he is old, he is still in good health.
⇒ **Despite** his old age, he is still in good health.

[핵심 37] 접속사의 종류

구분	표현	의미
1	명령문 ~ **and** …	~해라 그러면 …할 것이다 = **if**
	Work hard, **and** you will succeed in your job. = **If** you work hard, you will succeed in your job.	
2	명령문 ~ **or** …	~해라 그렇지 않으면 …할 것이다. = if + not = unless
	Hurry up, **or** you will not catch the first train. = **If** you **don't** hurry up, you will not catch the first train. = **Unless** you hurry up, you will not catch the first train.	
3	**if**	만약 ~라면, ~인지 아닌지(= whether)
	If you want to be a leader, you must have a leadership. I don't know **if** he will come here tonight.	

구분	표현	의미
4	**unless**	만약 ~하지 않는다면
	Unless you work hard, you can never succeed.	
5	**though, although, even though, even if**	비록 ~일지라도, ~임에도 불구하고
	Although he is very poor, he likes to help other people.	
6	**as**	~할 때, ~ 때문에, ~함에 따라서
	As he was young, he learned to swim with his mother. **As** he often lies, I don't like him. **As** she grew older, she became more silent.	

[핵심 38] 등위상관접속사

구분	표현	의미
1	Both A and B	A와 B 둘 다 (동사는 **복수**기준)
	Both he and I are right. 그와 나 둘 다 옳다.	
2	Either A or B	A와 B 둘 중 하나 (동사는 **B**기준)
	Either he or I am right. 그와 나 둘 중 한 사람만 옳다.	
3	Neither A nor B	A와 B 둘 다 아니다 (동사는 **B**기준)
	Neither he nor I am right. 그와 나 둘 다 옳지 않다.	
4	Not A but B	A가 아니라 B이다 (동사는 **B**기준)
	Not he but I am right. 그가 아니라 내가 옳다.	
5	Not only A but also B	A뿐만 아니라 B도 역시 (동사는 **B**기준)
	Not only he but also I am right. 그뿐만 아니라 나도 역시 옳다.	
6	B as well as A	A뿐만 아니라 B도 역시 (동사는 **B**기준)
	I as well as he am right. 그뿐만 아니라 나도 역시 옳다.	

[핵심 39] 전치사의 주요개념

- [전치사 + (대)명사/ 동명사] = 형용사구 혹은 부사구의 역할을 한다.

· The moon **in the sky** is bright.

· The moon is bright **in the sky.**

· This typewriter **is of no use.**

· Make yourself **at home.**

· He goes **to school on foot in the morning.**

<table>
<tr><td rowspan="3">전치사</td><td rowspan="3">+</td><td>명사</td><td></td></tr>
<tr><td>대명사</td><td>반드시 목적격을 쓴다.</td></tr>
<tr><td>동명사</td><td>동사가 올 때 동사원형 + ing(동명사)로 바꾼다.</td></tr>
</table>

· I am proud of <u>my mother</u>. (명사)

· I am proud of <u>him</u>. (대명사)

· I am proud of <u>winning</u> the game. (동명사)

[핵심 40] 주요 전치사 정리

구분	표현	예시
1	until(= till) : ~까지 (계속)	I will wait for you here **until** tomorrow.
	by : ~까지 (완료)	You must come home **by** ten.
2	before : ~전에	You must go there **before** dark.
	after : ~후에	He came back **after** a few hours.
3	from : ~부터 (시간의 출발점)	He will live here **from** next month.
	since : ~이래로 (시간의 계속)	He has lived here **since** last year.

구분	표현	예시
4	for : ~동안 (+ 숫자 + 시간명사)	He has studied English **for** three hours.
	during : ~동안 (+ 시간명사)	I went to the resort **during** summer vacation.
5	between : ~사이에 (둘 사이)	The post office lies **between** a bookstore and a hospital.
	among : ~사이에 (셋 이상)	Many birds are singing **among** the trees.
6	of : 물리적 변화	The desk is made **of** wood.
	from : 화학적 변화	Butter is made **from** milk.
7	for : ~에 찬성하는	I am **for** the opinion. (= in favor of)
	against : ~에 반대하는	I am **against** the opinion.

※ [1~5] 다음 (　　) 안에서 알맞은 말을 고르시오.

1. Please come to my house (during, while) you are in Busan.

2. He became wiser (as, unless) he grew older.

3. The author writes (both, either) a novel and an essay.

4. We'll go camping tomorrow (if, unless) the weather is bad.

5. You'll have another chance (that, even if) you failed this time.

※ [6~10] 다음 빈칸에 알맞은 것을 고르시오.

6. James was doing the dishes _______ I was cleaning the house.

① after　② until　③ while　④ before

7. 내 부탁을 들어 주면 네가 하라는 거 뭐든지 할게.
→ __________ you do me a favor, I'll do whatever you say.

① Although　② Unless
③ If　④ While

8. 민수는 운동을 잘하긴 하지만 자전거 타기를 무서워한다.

→ ____________ Minsu is good at sports, he is afraid of riding a bicycle.

① Although ② Whether

③ However ④ If

9. _______ Kim and Jung are satisfied with the exam results.

① Nor ② Both ③ Either ④ Not only

10. Neither David _______ Brian is good at running.

① or ② but ③ nor ④ and

02. 생활영어

02 생활영어

[유형 1] 일상 묻고 답하기

01 대화의 빈칸에 들어갈 알맞은 것을 고르시오.

A : Can I help you, ma'am?
B : Yes, I'd like to return this sweater.
A : What's the matter with it?
B : ______________________

① Here's $15.
② That sounds great.
③ It has a hole in it.
④ That's fine with me.

02 대화의 빈칸에 들어갈 알맞은 것을 고르시오.

A : Excuse me, can you show me a sweater?
B : Okay. How about this red one?
A : It's pretty. Is it on sale?
B : ______________ The sale is only for pants.

① Of course.
② Yes, please.
③ I don't mind.
④ I'm afraid not.

정답 | 1. ③ 2. ④

03 대화의 빈칸에 들어갈 말로 적절하지 않은 것은?

A : You always keep your words. I think that's great.

B : Thank you for saying that.

A : ______________________

① My pleasure.
② Not exactly.
③ Don't mention it.
④ You are welcome.

04 대화의 빈칸에 들어갈 알맞은 것을 고르시오.

A : King Hotel. May I help you?

B : Yes, I'd like to speak to Bill in room 301.

A : ______________________

① Pass me the salt, please.
② It took 3 days to get there.
③ I hope your dream come true.
④ Hold on please. I'll connect you.

05 대화의 빈칸에 들어갈 알맞은 것을 고르시오.

A : Did you have a nice vacation?

B : Terrible.

A : ________?

B : I stayed home and studied for my exam.

① Why ② Who ③ When ④ Which

정답 | 3. ② 4. ④ 5. ①

06 대화의 빈칸에 들어갈 알맞은 것을 고르시오.

A : Let's go see a movie together tomorrow.
B : Sounds great! What time shall we make it?
A : ____________________

① Three times a day.
② It opened yesterday.
③ Let's meet at nine o'clock.
④ I've seen the movie twice.

[유형 2] 의도 파악하기

07 대화에서 B의 의도로 알맞은 것은?

A : Don't you think we eat too much junk food?
B : <u>I couldn't agree more</u>.

① 동의 ② 제안 ③ 비난 ④ 충고

08 대화에서 밑줄 친 부분의 의도로 알맞은 것은?

A : I'm not good at English. Could you give me some advice?
B : Why don't you watch English DVDs?
A : That sounds good. <u>I appreciate your advice</u>.

① 축하 ② 감사 ③ 칭찬 ④ 충고

정답 | 6. ③ 7. ① 8. ②

09 대화에서 밑줄 친 부분의 의도로 알맞은 것은?

> A : What are you doing this Saturday?
> B : Nothing special.
> A : <u>How about going to the swimming pool</u>?

① 동의 ② 제안 ③ 의심 ④ 칭찬

10 밑줄 친 문장의 의도로 알맞은 것은?

> A : <u>You did a good job</u>! I like your speech.
> B : Thanks a lot.

① 칭찬하기 ② 소개하기
③ 상담하기 ④ 비난하기

11 대화에서 밑줄 친 부분의 의도로 알맞은 것은?

> A : I broke up with my girl friend.
> B : <u>Sorry to hear that, but cheer up</u>.

① 예약하기 ② 위로하기
③ 초청하기 ④ 칭찬하기

12 밑줄 친 말의 의도로 알맞은 것은?

> A : <u>Will you do me a favor</u>?
> B : Sure. What can I do for you?

① 부탁하기 ② 사과하기
③ 불평하기 ④ 칭찬하기

정답 | 9. ② 10. ① 11. ② 12. ①

13 다음 대화에서 밑줄 친 말의 의도로 알맞은 것은?

> A : This is how to prove it. <u>Are you with me</u>?
> B : Yes, I am. That's not so difficult.

① 사과하기　　② 확인하기
③ 허락하기　　④ 거절하기

14 밑줄 친 말의 의도로 가장 알맞은 것은?

> A : You can use my computer if you want to.
> B : Thanks. <u>I'm very grateful for your kindness</u>.

① 사과하기　　② 제안하기
③ 보고하기　　④ 감사하기

정답 | 13. ② 14. ④

[유형 3] 관계 / 장소 파악하기

(1) post office(우체국) : stamp(우표), postcard(엽서), package/parcel(소포), airmail (항공우편), scale(저울)

(2) airport(공항), airplane(비행기) : passport(여권), gate(탑승구), flight number(항공 편 번호), window/aisle seat(창가/통로 쪽 좌석), departure time(출발 시각), destination(목적지), one-way(편도), round trip(왕복), land(착륙하다), take off (이륙하다), delay(지연되다), check in(탑승 수속을 하다)
What's the purpose of your visit? - 방문 목적이 무엇인지요?

(3) library(도서관), bookstore(서점) : kind(종류), section(구역), shelf(선반), ID card(신분증), due(기한), borrow(빌리다), take out(대출하다), return(반납하다)

(4) bank(은행) : cash(현금), check(수표), account number(계좌번호), exchange(환전하다)

(5) hospital(병원), drugstore, pharmacy(약국) : medicine(약), pill(알약), prescription(처방전), shot(주사), toothache(치통), dentist(치과의사), headache(두통), cough(기침), fever(열), stomachache(복통), symptom(증상), sore throat(인후통)

(6) restaurant(식당) : order(주문), meal(식사), dessert(후식), bill/check(계산서), receipt(영수증), steak(스테이크)
I will treat you. – 제가 대접할게요.
Let's go Dutch. – 각자 부담합시다.

(7) taxi(택시) : Where would you like to go? - 어디로 가시겠습니까?
Here we are. - 다 왔습니다. / What's the fare? - 요금이 얼마지요?
Keep the change. - 거스름돈은 가지세요.

(8) store, shop(상점) :
What can I do for you? / How can I help you? - 무엇을 도와 드릴까요?
How do you like this one? - 이것은 어떻습니까?
I'm just looking around. - 그냥 둘러보고 있습니다.
Can I try it on? - 그것을 입어 봐도 될까요?
I'll take it. - 그것으로 살게요.

15 대화에서 두 사람의 관계로 가장 알맞은 것은?

A : Hi, Tom. What's wrong?

B : I have a terrible headache.

A : Let me check. Don't worry. It's not so serious.
Here is the prescription.

① 의사 – 환자 ② 기자 – 배우
③ 점원 – 고객 ④ 경찰 – 범인

16 대화에서 두 사람의 관계로 알맞은 것은?

A : May I see your passport?

B : Here you are.

A : Are you here for business or pleasure?

B : For pleasure.

① 약사 – 환자 ② 택시운전사 – 승객
③ 판매원 – 고객 ④ 입국심사원 – 여행객

17 대화에서 두 사람의 관계로 가장 알맞은 것은?

A : Sam's Restaurant. May I help you?

B : Yes. Can I make a reservation for Sunday?

A : Certainly. For what time?

B : 7 o'clock.

① 의사 – 환자 ② 기자 – 배우
③ 지배인 – 손님 ④ 수리공 – 주인

정답 | 15. ① 16. ④ 17. ③

18 대화에서 두 사람의 관계로 가장 알맞은 것은?

A : May I help you?
B : When is the earliest flight for Boston?
A : It's at 6:10.
B : Then I'd like a ticket to Boston.

① 경찰관 – 행인
② 택시 운전사 – 승객
③ 식당 지배인 – 손님
④ 항공사 직원 – 손님

19 대화에서 두 사람의 관계로 가장 알맞은 것은?

A : May I take your order, please?
B : Yes, I'd like spaghetti with tomato sauce.

① 의사 – 환자
② 사장– 직원
③ 은행원 – 고객
④ 식당 종업원 – 손님

20 다음 대화에서 두 사람의 관계로 가장 알맞은 것은?

A : Hello? Can I help you?
B : Yes. I'm calling to reserve a single room.
A : Sure. How long do you want to stay?
B : For six nights.

① 경찰 – 시민
② 교수 – 학생
③ 호텔직원 – 고객
④ 택시기사 – 승객

정답 | 18. ④ 19. ④ 20. ③

21 대화가 이루어지는 장소로 가장 알맞은 것은?

A : How can I help you?
B : Could I have five 40-cent stamps, please.
A : Of course. Anything else?
B : Yes. How much is a postcard to Germany?
A : Fifty cents.

① In an airport
② In a post office
③ In a police station
④ In a department store

22 대화가 이루어지는 장소로 가장 알맞은 것은?

A : May I help you?
B : I would like to exchange Korean wons for US dollars.
A : How much do you want?
B : Thirty dollars.

① In a bank
② In a theater
③ In a restaurant
④ In a coffee shop

23 대화가 이루어지는 장소로 가장 알맞은 것은?

A : Fill her up, please.
B : Yes, regular or premium?
A : Regular, please.

① At a bank
② At a hospital
③ At a gas station
④ At a post office

정답 | 21. ② 22. ① 23. ③

24 대화가 이루어지는 장소로 가장 알맞은 것은?

A : May I help you?
B : Yes, I'm looking for a shirt.
A : Are you looking for a particular design?
B : Not really, but I think red one would be nice.

① At a bank ② At a police station
③ At a hospital ④ At a clothing store

25 대화가 이루어지는 장소로 가장 알맞은 것은?

A : Can I borrow a book now?
B : Of course. Which one do you want to read this time?
A : I'd like to try a science novel today.
B : Let's see. Oh, here's a good one.

① 사진관 ② 도서관 ③ 운동장 ④ 동물원

26 대화가 이루어지는 장소로 가장 알맞은 것은?

A : Are these books on sale?
B : Yes, all of these are four dollars each.
A : Do you have books of travel?
B : Yes, they are on the second floor.

① 서점 ② 식당 ③ 세탁소 ④ 옷가게

정답 | 24. ④ 25. ② 26. ①

[유형 4] 제안, 부탁, 권유, 초대하기

27 대화의 빈칸에 들어갈 말로 적절하지 않은 것은?

A : These books are so heavy. ________________

B : Sure, I'd like to.

① Help me, please.
② I need your help.
③ I'm not sure.
④ Can you give me a hand?

28 대화에서 빈칸에 알맞은 것은?

A : How can I get information about the World Cup?

B : ______________ That's the best way.

① Take some rest.
② Get some exercise.
③ Clean the bicycle.
④ Search on the Internet.

29 다음 대화에서 빈칸에 들어갈 알맞은 표현을 고르시오.

A : You look tired. What's the matter?

B : I have sleep problems. What should I do?

A : ______________________________

① I'm glad you slept well last night.
② Thank you for buying me this comfortable bed.
③ You should take a warm bath before going to bed.
④ I have something to do, so I cannot go to bed now.

정답 ꒐ 27. ③ 28. ④ 29. ③

30 대화에서 빈칸에 가장 알맞은 것은?

A : Please, help yourself to the cake.
B : ______________ I've had enough.

① Certainly. ② Yes, please.
③ No, thank you. ④ You're welcome.

31 다음 대화에서 빈칸에 들어갈 알맞은 표현을 고르시오.

A : I lost my watch on the subway.
B : That's too bad. ____________________
A : Thanks. I will.

① Maybe next time.
② What are you interested in?
③ How can I get to the post office?
④ How about checking the lost-and-found?

32 다음 대화에서 빈칸에 들어갈 알맞은 표현을 고르시오.

A : Jane, shall we go to the park?
B : _________________ I have to finish my homework.
A : All right. Maybe next time.

① I'm afraid I can't.
② I agree with you.
③ Certainly, I'd like to.
④ You did a good job.

정답 | 30. ③ 31. ④ 32. ①

[유형 5] 대화의 순서 파악하기

33 주어진 글에 이어질 대화의 순서로 알맞은 것은?

Good morning. What's the problem?

(A) Anything else?
(B) I have a stomachache and fever.
(C) No, that's all.

① (A) - (B) - (C)
② (B) - (A) - (C)
③ (C) - (A) - (B)
④ (C) - (B) - (A)

34 주어진 글에 이어질 대화의 순서로 알맞은 것은?

What are you interested in?

(A) Then how about joining the movie club?
(B) That's a good idea.
(C) I'm interested in movies.

① (A) - (B) - (C)
② (B) - (A) - (C)
③ (B) - (C) - (A)
④ (C) - (A) - (B)

35 (A)에 이어질 대화의 순서로 알맞은 것은?

(A) Why don't we go swimming this Saturday?

(B) Well, I am not good at swimming.
(C) Good. Thanks.
(D) Don't worry. I can help you.

① (B) - (D) - (C)
② (C) - (D) - (B)
③ (D) - (B) - (C)
④ (D) - (C) - (B)

정답 | 33. ② 34. ④ 35. ①

36 다음에 이어질 대화의 순서로 알맞은 것은?

Which club are you going to join?

(A) Why do you like that one?
(B) I'd like to join the Magic Club.
(C) Because I want to learn some magic tricks.

① (A) - (B) - (C)
② (B) - (A) - (C)
③ (C) - (A) - (B)
④ (C) - (B) - (A)

37 주어진 말에 이어질 대화의 순서로 알맞은 것은?

Did you hear the news?

(A) Oh! That's incredible.
(B) Our soccer team won the game.
(C) What news?

① (A) - (B) - (C)
② (B) - (A) - (C)
③ (B) - (C) - (A)
④ (C) - (B) - (A)

38 주어진 글에 이어질 두 사람의 대화 순서로 가장 알맞은 것은?

What's the purpose of your visit?

(A) How long are you staying here?
(B) About two weeks.
(C) I'm here on vacation.

① (A) - (C) - (B)
② (B) - (A) - (C)
③ (B) - (C) - (A)
④ (C) - (A) - (B)

정답 | 36. ② 37. ④ 38. ④

[유형 6] 의문사에 맞는 답하기

39 다음 대화의 빈칸에 알맞지 <u>않은</u> 것은?

A : How often do you read newspaper?
B : ____________.

① Never
② Every day
③ Once a week
④ For an hour

40 다음 대화의 빈칸에 알맞은 것은?

A : Who is your best friend?
B : It's Minsu.
A : ____________________?
B : He is tall with long hair.

① How old is he
② Where is he from
③ What does he look like
④ When does he arrive here

41 다음 대화의 빈칸에 알맞은 것은?

A : Long time no see. Where have you been?
B : I have been to Italy.
A : ________________________?
B : I went there on business.

① Where did you go
② Why did you go there
③ When did you go there
④ With whom did you go there

정답 | 39. ④ 40. ③ 41. ②

42 다음 대화의 빈칸에 들어갈 말로 가장 알맞은 것은?

A : ______________________?
B : I'm going to visit my friend in America.

① What does it look like
② What kind of sports do you like
③ What do you want to be in the future
④ What are you going to do this summer

43 다음 대화의 빈칸에 가장 알맞은 것은?

A : Which fruit do you like better, bananas or grapes?
B : _________________.

① I hope so
② No, you can't go
③ Yes, I will
④ I like grapes better

44 다음 대화의 빈칸에 들어갈 말로 가장 알맞은 것은?

A : ____________________________?
B : It takes 10 minutes by bus from here.

① What do you do for a living
② Who do you think is the smartest
③ How much do you pay for your cooking lessons
④ How long does it take to get to the art gallery

정답 | 42. ④ 43. ④ 44. ④

[유형 7] 심정 파악하기

45 다음 대화에서 알 수 있는 A의 심경으로 적절한 것은?

A : Finally, I've passed the test for a driver's license.
I'm so happy.
B : Congratulations!

① angry ② glad
③ sad ④ worried

46 다음 대화에서 알 수 있는 A의 심경으로 가장 알맞은 것은?

A : Look at this! I got opera tickets for free.
B : Really? How is that possible?
A : I won them at the quiz. I'm so happy.

① sad ② upset
③ bored ④ excited

47 다음 대화에서 알 수 있는 B의 심경으로 가장 알맞은 것은?

A : What's the matter with you?
B : I didn't do well in the speech contest.
A : Come on! You can do better next time.

① bored ② excited
③ satisfied ④ disappointed

정답 | 45. ② 46. ④ 47. ④

48 다음 대화에서 알 수 있는 A의 심경으로 가장 알맞은 것은?

A : I shouldn't have bought a cap.
B : Do you mean you don't like the cap?
A : I don't need it.
I should have been more careful when spending money.

① bored ② joyful
③ scared ④ regretful

49 다음 대화에서 알 수 있는 A의 심경으로 가장 알맞은 것은?

A : Mom, I won the first prize in the singing contest.
B : Wow, you did it. Congratulations!
A : I am very happy about that.

① excited ② fearful
③ regretful ④ depressed

50 다음 대화에서 알 수 있는 A의 심경으로 가장 알맞은 것은?

A : I am finally going to New Zealand.
B : Great! It's a very beautiful country.
A : Yes, I'm really glad to go there!

① sad ② upset
③ happy ④ gloomy

정답 | 48. ④ 49. ① 50. ③

1. 다음 빈칸에 들어갈 말로 적당하지 않은 것은?

> A : What's your e-mail address?
> B : Angel2019@korea.com.
> A : ______________________
> B : It's Angel2019@korea.com.

① Are you with me? ② I'm sorry?
③ Pardon me? ④ Could you say that again?

2. 다음 대화의 빈칸에 가장 적절한 것은?

> A : Mozart was born in Germany.
> B : ______________________
> Mozart was born in Austria.

① I think you are right.
② I'm sorry to hear that.
③ You can say that again.
④ I'm afraid that's not true.

3. 다음 대화에서 Tom이 Jane에게 권하는 것은?

> Tom : Would you like a taco?
> Jane : A taco? What is it?
> Tom : A taco is a Mexican food.
> It has beef and vegetables in it. Try one.
> Jane : OK. Um, it's really delicious.

① 타코 만들기 ② 타코 맛보기
③ 멕시코 여행하기 ④ 멕시코 요리 배우기

4. 다음 중 대화가 <u>어색한</u> 것은?

① A : What time shall we meet?
   B : Can you make it at five?
② A : I'm going to ride my bike.
   B : Be sure to wear a helmet.
③ A : You look upset. Why the long face?
   B : I won the baseball game.
④ A : Excuse me. I'm looking for a blouse.
   B : How about this green one?

5. 두 사람의 대화가 자연스럽게 이어지도록 배열한 것은?

(A) It was great. Do you mind my borrowing some more DVDs?
(B) Thanks a lot. I'll come to your house this weekend.
(C) How was the movie DVD I lent you yesterday?
(D) Of course not. Feel free to come anytime.

① (C)-(A)-(D)-(B)
② (C)-(B)-(A)-(D)
③ (D)-(A)-(B)-(C)
④ (D)-(C)-(A)-(B)

6. 다음 대화의 빈칸에 가장 알맞은 것은?

A : Excuse me. Can you help me?
B : Sure. What's the matter?
A : I've lost my wallet.
B : ______________________
Let me take you to the Lost and Found Department.
A : I appreciate your help.
B : Don't mention it.

① You did a good job.
② That's very exciting.
③ I'm glad to hear that.
④ I'm sorry to hear that.

7. 다음 대화를 읽고, 빈칸에 들어갈 표현이 순서대로 짝지어진 것을 고르면?

A : What are you going to do when you finish school?
B : I'm going to be an announcer.
A : Sounds great! How are you going to achieve your dream?
B : First, I will try to imitate good announcers.
A : What else are you going to do?
B : Second, I will ____________ so that I will be well-informed.
Third, I will ____________ so that I can communicate with foreigners.
A : I'm sure you'll be a great announcer in the future.

① get up early – go to the movies
② get up early – isten to the radio
③ read lots of books – learn foreign languages
④ read lots of books – go to the movies

8. 다음 대화에서 빈칸에 가장 적절한 것은?

A : Hi. What are you doing here in the basement?
B : I need to move this box to the other room.
A : It looks very heavy.
B : Yes, it is. ________________
A : No problem.

① Where can I move it?
② Can you give me a hand?
③ What brings you here?
④ What do you want me to do?

9. 다음 전화 통화에서 빈칸에 들어갈 말로 가장 적절한 것은?

A : Hello, Mom! I've just arrived here in Chicago.
B : Steve, how is the weather there?
A : It's snowing outside. And the wind is strong.
The temperature has dropped to ten degrees below zero.
B : That cold? Make sure to put on warm clothes.
A : I will, Mom. And what's the weather like in Seoul?
B : ______________________________

① I like warm weather with clear skies. So spring is my favorite.
② The weatherman said there would be heavy snow in Chicago.
③ I like Seoul better than Chicago because of the weather.
④ It has been raining for three days. I hope it will clear up soon.

10. 다음 밑줄 친 부분 대신에 쓸 수 있는 말로 가장 알맞은 것은?

A : Did you see Mary today?
B : Yes. But why did she <u>have such a long face</u>?
A : I have no idea.
B : I thought she'd be happy.
A : Yeah, especially since she bought a new car.
B : Maybe it's some kind of personal problem.

① look unhappy
② look too big
③ lose her way
④ save her face

11. 다음 대화의 빈칸에 들어갈 표현으로 알맞은 것을 고르면?

A : What can I do for you?
B : I'm looking for a jacket for myself.
A : How about this blue one?
B : It looks nice. ____________________
A : Sure. Go ahead.
(After while)
B : I think it looks good on me. I'll take it.

① How do I look?
② How much is it?
③ Can I try it on?
④ Can you try it on?

12. 다음 대화에서 두 사람이 처해 있는 상황은?

A : This is why I don't like to live in a big city.
B : I understand you. Every day, the traffic is heavy.
A : Whew, this morning, it's more terrible!
It'll take more than 2 hours to get to the office.
What if we may run out of gas in the middle?
B : Don't worry. I think it's enough.
A : We'd better take a subway tomorrow.

① 속도 위반
② 교통 혼잡
③ 주차 위반
④ 연료 부족

13. 다음 대화의 빈칸에 가장 적절한 것을 고르시오.

A : Long time no see, Jane. How have you been?
B : Fine, thanks. And you?
A : Great. By the way, how is your family?
B : Very well, thank you.
A : Please say hello to your family.
B : ______________________

① That's all. ② OK, I will.
③ You're welcome. ④ You're wrong.

14. 다음 대화의 빈칸에 들어갈 알맞은 것은?

A : Excuse me, would you show me the way to the bookstore?
B : Sure. Go down this road one block and turn left at the corner.
A : Turn left at the corner?
B : Yes. You'll find it on your right. ________________
A : Thank you very much.

① Congratulations! ② You're welcome.
③ Long time no see. ④ You can't miss it.

15. 다음 짝지어진 대화가 서로 어울리지 <u>않는</u> 것은?

① A : May I take your order?
B : Yes, I'd like an apple pie.
② A : What's your favorite subject?
B : I like English best.
③ A : What time shall we meet?
B : At the pizza house.
④ A : Is it OK if I open the window?
B : No problem.

16. 다음 대화의 빈칸에 가장 적절한 것은?

A : Hello.
B : Hello. May I speak to David?
A : Speaking. ________________
B : This is Minho.

① Who's calling, please?
② What are you doing?
③ When are you leaving?
④ May I leave a message?

17. 다음 중 두 사람의 대화가 자연스럽지 <u>않은</u> 것은?

① A : I'm sorry for being late.
B : You're welcome.
② A : Have some more coffee?
B : No, thank you.
③ A : Can you cross the river?
B : I'm afraid I can't.
④ A : Have you ever been to New York?
B : No, but I'd like to go.

18. 다음 대화의 빈칸에 가장 적절한 것은?

A : How can I help you?
B : I'd like to get some information about a flight.
A : Do you know what the flight number is?
B : That's BA 606. What time will it land at the airport?
A : ________________________

① Thank you for your information.
② My seat number is 15D.
③ What time do we leave?
④ The arrival time is 10:30 p.m.

19. 다음 대화의 빈칸에 들어갈 대답으로 적절한 것을 고르면?

> A : Oh no. Another traffic jam!
> We might be late for the concert.
> B : Don't worry. Once we get around this corner, it'll be okay.
> A : I hope so. How much time do we have before the show starts?
> B : ________________________________

① I usually take the bus to work.
② We still have forty minutes left.
③ Sure, the concert will be exciting.
④ Please watch out at the next corner.

20. 다음 대화의 빈칸에 들어갈 대답으로 적절한 것을 고르면?

> A : Excuse me, I bought this book here last week, but there is a problem with it.
> B : What's the problem?
> A : Look here. Some of the pages were not printed.
> B : ________________________________

① Sorry, let me exchange it for another one.
② I'm afraid that our printer is out of order.
③ Yes, the novel was a best-seller once.
④ We really appreciate your purchase.

21. 두 사람이 하는 대화의 주제로 가장 적절한 것을 고르면?

A : Irene, what are you reading?
B : Hi, Tom. Look at this article in our school magazine about doctors.
A : What does it say?
B : It says one-third of medical school graduates are women.
A : No doubt. I have seen many women in medical schools.
B : Wow, women account for over 40% of all doctors.
A : My sister is actually a doctor.
She has a lot of female doctor friends, too.
B : Female doctors will be the majority soon.
A : It certainly looks that way.
B : I think, it's a positive trend for women.

① 변화하는 대학 교육
② 여성 의사의 증가 추세
③ 여성 의료 전문 변호사의 역할
④ 의사들에게 요구되는 전문성

22. 두 사람의 관계를 가장 잘 나타낸 것을 고르면?

A : Hi, Ms. Han. Congratulations! Your show in Italy was very impressive.
B : Thank you very much.
A : I'm going to write an article about your work for our newspaper.
B : Thank you. I'm quite honored.
A : How did you like the show?
B : I'm happy because I had the opportunity to present my philosophy on clothes in Italy.
A : So, what is your philosophy?
B : For me, clothes are culture, and I want to share Korean beauty with the world through Hanbok.
A : Korean beauty! That's great.
What plans do you have for the near future?
B : I'll have similar events in other European countries.
A : Good luck!
Ms. Han, lastly for our readers, may I take a picture of you?
B : Sure, it would be my pleasure.

① 무대 감독 – 연기자
② 옷가게 주인 – 고객
③ 기자 – 의상 디자이너
④ 사진사 – 모델

23. 다음 대화에서 B가 봉사활동에 갈 수 없는 이유를 고르면?

A : Thank goodness! Midterm exams are over.
B : Yes. I feel like I'm walking on air.
Do you have any plans this Saturday, Lisa?
A : I'm going to do some volunteer work at an animal shelter.
B : What are you supposed to do there?
A : I'm going to help feed the cats and dogs. It'll be fun.
Do you want to join me?
B : It sounds really interesting, but I can't go.
A : Why not? Do you have something to do this Saturday?
B : No, I'll be free, but I'm allergic to animal hair.
A : I'm sorry to hear that.
Next time, let's go somewhere else like a library, instead.
B : Sounds good.

① 중간고사 준비를 해야 해서
② 동물원 구경을 하러 가야 해서
③ 동물 털 알레르기 때문에
④ 도서관에 가야 해서

24. 여자가 남자에게 부탁한 일로 가장 적절한 것을 고르면?

W : What time will your parents be here, honey?
M : They will arrive in an hour.
Afterwards, why don't we treat them to dinner at a nice restaurant?
W : But I think they will be tired because of their long drive.
So, I want to cook a special dinner for them, instead.
M : All right, but I'm afraid you don't have enough time.
W : How about Bulgogi? That doesn't take much time to make.
And we have fresh beef.
M : That's a good choice. Do we have vegetables?
W : Not enough. Could you go and get some at the market?
M : Sure. Should I pick up some fruits as well?
W : No, your parents said they were bringing some.
M : All right. I'll be back soon.

① 식당 예약하기
② 소고기 사 오기
③ 채소 사 오기
④ 부모님 마중 나가기

25. 호텔 예약에 관해 두 사람이 언급하지 않은 것을 고르면?

[Telephone rings]

A : Good morning, Healing Spa Hotel. How may I help you?

B : I'd like to make a reservation.
I got an e-mail saying your hotel has a special offer.

A : Yes, ma'am. This month, if you stay for 2 nights, we'll give you a third night for free.

B : Good. I'd like to book a double room from the 20th to the 23rd.

A : That would be for three nights, right?

B : Yes. Do you have a room with an ocean view?

A : Let me check. [pause] Yes.
But, we only have one left during that period.
It's $100 per night including tax.

B : It sounds reasonable. I'll reserve the room. When can I check in?

A : You can check in after 3p.m.

B : Great! See you then.

① 특별 혜택
② 투숙 기간
③ 객실 전망
④ 퇴실 시간

26. B가 지불할 총금액은 얼마인지 고르면?

A : Good afternoon. Can I help you?
B : Yes, please. I would like to buy some gifts for friends.
A : How about this heart-shaped key chain?
B : It looks pretty. How much is it?
A : The original price was $4, but now, we are offering a 50% discount on this item.
B : OK. I'll take 5 key chains. Anything else you'd recommend?
A : Hmm… How about this refrigerator magnet?
It's a very popular item. It's $4.
B : But it's a bit expensive. Can I get a discount on this as well?
A : I'm afraid not because it's a brand-new item.
B : I see. Then let me have 3 magnets.
A : So you want to buy 5 key chains and 3 refrigerator magnets, right?
B : Exactly. Thanks.

① $18
② $22
③ $26
④ $32

27. 다음 대화의 빈칸에 들어갈 대답으로 가장 적절한 것은?

A : Why the long face, Susan? Did something happen at school?
B : Yeah, Dad. I had a quarrel with Julie.
A : Why? You normally get along with her.
B : She's a good friend, but sometimes she's a little rude to me.
A : Really? So, what did she do to make you so upset?
B : Actually, this time I'm upset with myself.
A : What do you mean?
B : I got angry and shouted, "I hate you!" at her.
A : That's not like you.
B : ______________________________

① I know. I shouldn't have done that.
② But don't you think she is nice?
③ You mean she needs to be more active?
④ Yeah, as you said, she doesn't like me.

28. 다음 대화의 빈칸에 들어갈 속담으로 가장 적절한 것은?

A : Did you think about where to go this weekend?
B : Mom, I'd like to go to Busan.
A : But Sumi said she would rather go skiing.
B : What do you think?
A : Well, actually I want to go hiking to the nearby mountain to enjoy the fresh air.
B : It's very hard to make a decision.
A : Right. ____________________

① Every dog has his day.
② Better late than never.
③ No news is good news.
④ So many men, so many minds.

29. 다음 대화를 나누는 두 사람의 관계로 가장 적절한 것은?

A : Excuse me! Are you John Smith?
B : Yes, I am. How do you know me?
A : I have read some famous books you wrote about raising children.
B : How nice! I hope they helped.
A : Can you sign your new book for me?
B : No problem!

① 감독 - 선수
② 교사 - 학생
③ 작가 - 독자
④ 배우 - 관객

30. 다음 그림의 상황에 가장 어울리는 대화를 고르면?

① M : You should turn your phone off in class.
W : I'm so sorry. I forgot to turn it off.
② M : It's 9:30. Why are you so late?
W : Sorry, but I was stuck in a traffic jam.
③ M : How may I help you?
W : I'm looking for a new smartphone.
④ M : May I speak to your mom?
W : No, she's not at home.

31. 다음 대화가 이루어지는 장소로 가장 알맞은 곳은?

> A : What can I do for you, ma'am?
> B : I want to get this coat dry-cleaned by tomorrow.
> A : Sure, no problem. Anything else?
> B : Can you wake me up in the morning?
> A : OK. What time should we call?
> B : At 6:30, please. When is check-out time?
> A : It's 12 o'clock.

① 공항 ② 은행 ③ 세탁소 ④ 호텔

32. 다음 대화에서 두 사람이 만날 시각은?

> A : Let's go to see a concert this Saturday.
> B : Sounds good! Who's playing?
> A : My cousin's band. It starts at 7:30 in the evening. Is that OK?
> B : Perfect! What time should we meet?
> A : Let's meet at 7:00.
> B : I think it's too late. We will only have half an hour before the concert starts. How about at 6:30?
> A : That sounds better. See you then.

① 6:00 p.m. ② 6:30 p.m. ③ 7:00 p.m. ④ 7:30 p.m.

33. 다음 대화에서 언급하지 않은 것은?

A : I'm sorry I'm late. Did I miss anything?
B : There was just an announcement about the theater's rules.
A : All right. What are the rules?
B : Well, you should not bring in any food.
A : That sounds easy enough. Is that all?
B : No. Cellphones must be turned off and animals are not allowed in the theater.
A : I see. Is it OK if I take a picture while watching the movie?
B : No way, of course not.

①

②

③

④

34. 다음 대화의 빈칸에 들어갈 대답으로 알맞은 것을 고르면?

A : Tomorrow is the day of my big race!
B : Really? What time does it begin?
A : It starts at 9 a.m. Can you be there?
B : Oh, I'm sorry but I'm busy tomorrow morning.
A : What are you going to do?
B : I have to help my brother paint his house.
A : Well, if you cannot come, please wish me luck.
B : ______________________

① I need your help.
② I can't believe it.
③ I'm sorry to hear that.
④ I hope you win the race.

35. 다음의 대화에서 A가 주문하려는 케이크를 고르시오.

A : I want to order a Christmas cake for my children.
B : Great! Which design do you want, a circle or a square?
A : Let me see. I want a circle.
B : Which decorations would you like? We have Santa, trees, or flowers.
A : I would like Santa.
B : Yes, ma'am. Do you want anything else?
A : I also want a message written on the cake. For example, I Love You.
B : Oh, that's a good idea.

①

②
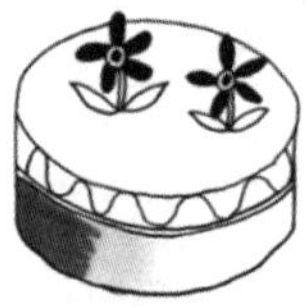

③

④

36. 다음의 대화를 나누는 두 사람의 관계로 적절한 것은?

A : Excuse me, I want to save my money.
B : Do you have an account?
A : No, I don't.
B : Then you have to open a new savings account.
A : OK. What do I need to open one?
B : You must submit your ID card.
A : Here it is. Is there anything else?
B : Just fill in this form, please.
A : Thanks a lot

① a model – a director
② a customer – a teller
③ a reporter – a police officer
④ a passenger – a flight attendant

37. 다음 대화가 이루어지는 장소로 가장 적절한 것은?

A : Good morning. Where do you want to go?
B : I would like to go to Incheon International Airport. How long will it take?
A : It will take about half an hour to drive to the airport.
Fasten your seat belt, please.
B : OK. My flight will depart at 10:30 a.m.
A : I see. How was your trip here in Korea?
B : Excellent! I especially liked the National Museum. It was very impressive.

① 공항 ② 박물관 ③ 택시 ④ 지하철

38. 다음 대화에서 두 사람이 만날 요일과 시간으로 알맞은 것은?

A : It's finally Friday! I have tickets for the play-off baseball game tomorrow.
B : Really? I'd love to go. Can I go with you?
A : Of course. The game starts at 4 p.m.
B : What time should we get there?
A : To make sure we get a good seat, we should be there one hour before the game.
B : Okay. Let's meet outside the stadium then.
A : Great. See you at Gate 1.

① Friday, 3 p.m. ② Friday, 4 p.m.
③ Saturday, 3 p.m. ④ Saturday, 4 p.m.

39. 다음 대화의 빈칸에 들어갈 대답으로 가장 적절한 것은?

A : Paul, the music is too loud. What are you doing?
B : Oh, sorry for bothering you. I'm practicing for a pop song contest.
A : Really? When is the contest?
B : This weekend.
A : What song are you going to sing?
B : I'm going to sing "You Raise Me Up".
A : Oh, I love that song.
B : Me, too. But I'm so nervous. I'm not sure if I can do well.
A : ______________________

① That's a good idea.
② Don't worry. You'll do a great job.
③ Thanks. It's nice of you to say do.
④ Sorry. I'm afraid I can't.

40. 다음 대화를 나누는 두 사람의 관계로 가장 적절한 것을 고르시오.

A : Excuse me, ma'am.
B : How may I help you, sir?
A : I really enjoyed today's exhibition.
B : Great! I'm very happy to hear that.
A : Whose paintings are you planning to display next?
B : We will be displaying Pablo Picasso's from next weekend.
A : Fantastic! He is my favorite artist. I won't miss it.

① 수강생 - 화가
② 의뢰인 - 변호사
③ 배우 - 감독
④ 관람객 - 미술관 직원

41. 다음 그림의 상황에 가장 어울리는 대화를 고르시오.

① A : What's the weather like today?
B : It's mild and sunny.
② A : Do you have a table for two?
B : Certainly, ma'am. Please come this way.
③ A : Excuse me. You can't take your dog into this store.
B : Really? I didn't know dogs are not allowed.
④ A : Honey, be careful while driving! It is raining heavily.
B : Okay. I'll slow down.

42. 두 사람이 대화를 나누는 장소로 가장 알맞은 곳은?

A : Good morning!
B : I booked a plane ticket to Seoul at 11:00 a.m.
A : Okay. Can I see your passport?
B : Here you go.
A : All right, I found your reservation.
B : By the way, can I get a window seat on the plane?
A : No problem. Your seat is 3A. Here is your boarding pass.
B : Thank you.
A : You're welcome. Enjoy your flight!

① 공항 ② 극장 ③ 서점 ④ 호텔

43. 다음 대화에서 B가 지불해야 할 총금액은 얼마인지 고르면?

A : Hello. How can I help you?
B : How much is it to ride the rail bike?
A : Ten dollars for each adult and five dollars for each child.
B : I thought children ride for free.
A : Well, it depends. How old is your child?
B : He is seven years old.
A : I'm sorry. Only children under five are free.
B : Then, 2 adult tickets and 1 child ticket, please.
A : Here you are.
B : Thank you.

① $5 ② $10 ③ $17 ④ $25

44. 다음 대화의 빈칸에 들어갈 대답으로 가장 적절한 것을 고르면?

> A : Hi, Jenny! Long time no see.
> B : Hi, Tom. Wow, is that a new bicycle?
> A : Yes, it is. What do you think about it?
> B : It's wonderful. It looks cool.
> A : I think so, too. My grandfather bought it for me.
> B : How kind of him! Is there any special reason?
> A : It's because I won first prize in my school essay contest.
> B : ______________________________

① Don't take it so hard.
② Congratulations! I envy you.
③ I hope you can find it soon.
④ I appreciate it. That'll be a great help.

45. 두 사람의 관계로 가장 적절한 것을 고르면?

> A : Good afternoon, Ms. Lee. I want to check out these books.
> B : Did you bring your ID card?
> A : Oh, no. I forgot to bring it.
> B : That's OK. What class are you in?
> A : Class 2.
> B : And your number in the class?
> A : My number in the class is nineteen.
> B : OK. Don't forget to return the books in two weeks.
> A : Sure. Thank you very much.
> B : Have a nice day!

① 투숙객 – 호텔 직원
② 학생 – 사서
③ 승객 – 승무원
④ 손님 – 점원

46. 다음 그림의 상황에 가장 어울리는 대화를 고르면?

① A : May I take your order?
B : Yes, two cheese burgers and two sodas, please.

② A : Hello. I am calling to talk to Frank.
B : I am sorry, but he is not at home right now.

③ A : Hello, how would you like your hair cut?
B : I'd like my hair short, please.

④ A : Good afternoon. How may I help you?
B : I would like to buy a baseball cap.

47. 두 사람이 대화를 나누는 장소로 가장 적절한 곳을 고르면?

A : Good afternoon.
B : Good afternoon. I want to have my picture taken.
A : What do you need the picture for?
B : I need it for my passport.
A : I see. How many pictures do you need?
B : Just five, please. Can I get them in an hour?
A : Of course. If you're ready, take a seat over there. We'll get started.

① 사진관　② 병원　③ 은행　④ 미술관

48. 다음 대화에서 딸이 아버지에게 부탁한 물건으로 언급되지 <u>않은</u> 것을 고르면?

A : I'm going to the store this afternoon. Do you need anything?
B : Yes, I need an eraser.
A : Anything else?
B : Umm. I need a pencil case and two notebooks.
A : OK. Is that all?
B : Oh, no! I totally forgot about my math homework.
A : Why don't you write down all the items you need?
B : No, it's not necessary. I just need a ruler and a glue stick.
A : OK, I got it. If you need something else, just give me a call.
B : Yes, Dad! Thank you.

① 지우개 ② 공책 ③ 가위 ④ 자

49. 다음 대화에서 B가 할 일로 가장 적절한 것을 고르면?

A : Hi, Jane. What are you reading?
B : 'The Future World.' This novel is very interesting.
A : You know what? The same story was made into a movie.
B : Oh, really? I want to see it.
A : Then, how about going to see that movie together this Saturday?
B : OK. I'm going to buy the tickets online.
A : Sounds good.
B : After watching the movie, let's have dinner together.
A : Great! Don't forget to buy the tickets.

① 외출하기 ② 책 주문하기
③ 작문 숙제하기 ④ 영화표 구매하기

50. 다음 대화의 빈칸에 들어갈 대답으로 가장 알맞은 것을 고르면?

A : Hi, Paul! What are you doing?
B : Hi, Susan! I'm working on a model airplane for my science class.
A : I thought it was due last Thursday.
B : Yes, but I didn't finish it in time.
A : Really? When is the next due date?
B : I have to finish it by tomorrow morning.
A : Tomorrow morning? I can help you.
B : ______________________

① I'd appreciate it.
② I forgot all about it.
③ I'm sorry to hear that.
④ I'm glad you finished it.

03

03. 독해
(유형별 해법 익히기)

03 독해(유형별 해법 익히기)

[유형 1] 빈칸 채우기

01 다음 글의 빈칸에 들어갈 말로 알맞은 것을 고르시오.

Seat belts __________ you in many ways. They extend the time it takes your body to stop. They make the change in speed less sudden and dangerous for your body.

① hurt
② protect
③ destroy
④ celebrate

words

extend 늘이다	**hurt** 상처입히다	**protect** 보호하다
destroy 파괴하다	**celebrate** 축하하다	

정답 : ②

02 다음 글의 빈칸에 들어갈 말로 알맞은 것을 고르시오.

A sense of control is the key to success. Optimists feel in control of their own lives. Even when things go wrong, their will remains strong. They try to look on the ________ side of things.

① tiny
② awful
③ bright
④ negative

words

a sense of control 통제력	**optimist** 낙천주의자	**in control of** ~을 통제하는
will 의지, 뜻	**remain** 남아있다	**tiny** 작은
awful 두려운	**negative** 부정적인	

정답 : ③

03 빈칸에 공통으로 들어갈 말로 가장 알맞은 것은?

A _______ is like a photo of our times and a time capsule of our history. If you want to keep up with the world around you, read a ______. Most ______ stories deal with straight facts.

① diary ② letter
③ newspaper ④ pamphlet

words

keep up with ~에 밝다, 뒤떨어지지 않다
deal with 다루다
straight fact 꾸밈없는 사실

정답 : ③

04 빈칸에 들어갈 말로 가장 알맞은 것은?

Some people do not eat particular food for ________ reasons. For example, Hindus do not eat beef because cows are considered holy animals. Jewish people and Moslems do not eat pork because pigs are thought to be unclean.

① religious ② technical
③ physical ④ economic

words

particular 특정한
holy 신성한
unclean 불결한
religious 종교적인
technical 기술적인
physical 신체적인
economic 경제적인

정답 : ①

[유형 2] 글의 목적 찾기

05 다음 글의 목적으로 가장 알맞은 것은?

If you are serious about being a cook, your parents will support you. They want you to be happy more than anything. You'd better talk to your parents about your dream.

① to complain
② to advise
③ to advertise
④ to apologize

words

serious 진지한, 심각한 **support** 지원(응원)하다 **complain** 불평하다
advertise 광고하다 **apologize** 사과하다

정답 : ②

06 다음 글을 쓴 목적으로 가장 알맞은 것은?

Dear Teacher
My son was late for school this morning because he didn't get out of bed until noon. His laziness is a big problem. Please tell me how I can break his bad habit.

① 감사 인사
② 고민 상담
③ 초청 거절
④ 취업 부탁

words

get out of bed 일어나다 **laziness** 게으름
break a habit 버릇을 고치다

정답 : ②

07 다음 글을 쓴 목적으로 가장 알맞은 것은?

> Dear Kevin
>
> My family is going to visit the Folk Village this weekend. I want you to come and join us. Do you have time on this Saturday? Let's have a great time together. Please let me know if you can come or not.

① to appreciate ② to encourage
③ to comfort ④ to invite

words

Folk Village 민속촌 **join** 함께 하다, 가입하다 **appreciate** 감사하다
encourage 격려하다 **comfort** 위로하다

정답 : ④

08 다음 글을 쓴 목적으로 가장 알맞은 것은?

> Our volunteer service center has many great activities for you. These activities give you a chance to help others. We hope to see you join us.

① 감사 ② 동의
③ 권유 ④ 항의

words

volunteer 자원봉사(하다)
activity 활동

정답 : ③

[유형 3] 글의 제목 찾기

09 다음 글의 제목으로 알맞은 것은?

Friendships need as much care as garden flowers. Good friendships involve careful listening, honesty, respect, and trust. Without these things, friendships are as weak as glass. However, with effort, friendships can become stronger than stone.

① How Flowers Die
② How Friendships Grow
③ How Honesty Pays
④ How Glass Breaks Down

words

care 관심, 보살핌
involve 수반(포함)하다
honesty 정직
respect 존경, 존중
trust 신뢰
effort 노력

정답 : ②

10 다음 글의 제목으로 가장 알맞은 것은?

My family had a trip to Australia last summer. We liked the beautiful beaches and the warm weather. We visited the Sydney Opera House. We had a good time.

① Beaches in Australia
② Weather of Sydney
③ Opera House in Sydney
④ Family Trip to Australia

words

trip 여행
Australia 오스트레일리아, 호주
weather 날씨

정답 : ④

11 다음 글의 제목으로 알맞은 것은?

It helps to talk to someone about your problem. Perhaps friends, family members, or teachers can help you see your problem in a different way. By sharing your problem, it can be solved easily.

① Read a Good Book
② Share Your Problem
③ Make a Lot of Money
④ Keep Your Room Clean

words

problem 문제
share 공유하다, 나누다
solve 풀다, 해결하다

정답 : ②

12 다음 글의 제목으로 가장 알맞은 것은?

There are many ways to save the environment. First, recycle a can. Then you can save enough energy to run a TV for two hours. Second, try to walk, ride a bike, or use a bus or a subway. Also, take a short shower. These can save the Earth.

① Take a Walk!
② Enjoy Your Life!
③ Brush Your teeth!
④ Help the Environment!

words

environment 환경
recycle 재활용하다
can 깡통, 통조림
run 작동시키다
ride (자전거, 차량을) 타다

정답 : ④

[유형 4] 글의 주제 찾기

13 다음 글의 주제로 가장 알맞은 것은?

Rain is a wonderful gift of nature. It helps to grow food in many areas of the world. This rainwater supports the life of human beings, animals and plants. With enough rain, you can drink water at home when you are thirsty.

① 비의 유용성
② 갈증 해소법
③ 농작물 재배
④ 빗물의 오염

words

gift 선물	**nature** 자연	**grow** 재배하다	**area** 지역
support 지탱(유지)하다	**human being** 인간	**plant** 식물	**thirsty** 목이 마른, 갈증이 나는

정답 : ①

14 인터넷에 관한 다음 글의 주제로 가장 알맞은 것은?

In cyberspace it is important to remember the other person. You should keep the same standard of behavior online that you follow in your life. This means that you should be thoughtful about other people and keep good manners when you are on the Net.

① 사용의 편리성
② 중독의 심각성
③ 접속의 용이성
④ 예절의 중요성

words

cyberspace 가상의 공간	**standard** 기준, 규범	**behavior** 행동, 태도
follow 따르다, 지키다	**thoughtful** 사려 깊은	**manners** 예절, 예의

정답 : ④

15 다음 글의 주제로 가장 알맞은 것은?

> Gift-giving customs and rules vary from culture to culture. If you send flowers in Europe, be sure to send them in odd numbers. In China, try to give things in pairs because Chinese culture stresses harmony and balance.

① 선물의 역사
② 선물하는 이유
③ 선물을 받는 즐거움
④ 선물하기의 문화적 차이

words

custom 관습, 풍습	**vary** 다르다, 달라지다	**culture** 문화
be sure to 꼭 ~해라	**odd number** 홀수	**in pairs** 짝을 지어
stress 강조하다	**harmony** 조화	**balance** 균형

정답 : ④

16 다음 글의 주제로 가장 알맞은 것은?

> Kevin is short, but he is proud that he can run fast. He knows who he is, how he looks and what he can do well. Although he sometimes experiences problems with his weakness, he doesn't accept it badly. He loves himself and takes pride in his abilities.

① 외모의 중요성
② 자신에 대한 존중감
③ 다양한 경험의 중요성
④ 호기심은 문제 해결의 시작

words

proud 자랑으로 여기는	**experience** 경험하다	**weakness** 약점
accept 받아들이다	**take pride in** ~을 자랑스러워하다	**ability** 능력

정답 : ②

[유형 5] 글의 요지 찾기

17 동물원에 대한 글의 요지로 알맞은 것은?

We are surprised to hear that a lion escaped from the zoo. We need more guards at the zoo to keep animals from running away. Besides, more guards are needed to provide safety for the public.

① 경비원 숫자를 늘려야 한다.
② 다른 장소로 이전해야 한다.
③ 관람 시간을 연장해야 한다.
④ 식물원도 함께 있어야 한다.

words

surprised 놀란
escape 탈출하다
guard 경비원
run away 달아나다
keep A from ~ing A가 ~하지 못하게 하다
provide 제공하다
besides 게다가

정답 : ①

18 다음 글의 요지로 알맞은 것은?

People may think that chocolate is okay for pets. However, chocolate can kill them. For example, a few weeks ago, a dog died after eating chocolate. I don't think that any pet owner wants to suffer the death of a pet. Therefore, you had better keep chocolate away from your pets.

① 버려지는 애완동물이 많다.
② 애완동물은 추위에 약하다.
③ 초콜릿은 영양분이 풍부하다.
④ 초콜릿은 애완동물에게 해롭다.

words

pet 애완동물
owner 주인, 소유자
suffer 경험하다, 괴로워하다
therefore 그러므로
had better ~하는 게 좋다

정답 : ④

19 다음 글의 요지로 가장 알맞은 것은?

Eating breakfast is very good for teenagers' learning. Many researchers have shown that students who eat breakfast do better in school than those who don't eat it.

① 비만은 청소년들의 건강에 해롭다.
② 학교의 적극적인 학습지도가 필요하다.
③ 학생들의 학습량이 학업성취에 영향을 미친다.
④ 아침밥을 먹는 것이 학생들의 학습에 도움이 된다.

words

be good for ~에 좋다 **teenager** 십대, 청소년 **learning** 학습
researcher 연구원

정답 : ④

20 다음 글의 요지로 가장 알맞은 것은?

Animals can predict weather changes. Birds fly much lower right before it rains. Also, black bears stay in deeper caves when they expect a very cold winter.

① 인간은 자연재해를 극복할 수 있다.
② 많은 동물이 멸종위기에 처해 있다.
③ 동물은 인간의 도움 없이 살 수 없다.
④ 동물은 날씨의 변화를 예측할 수 있다.

words

predict 예측(예상)하다 **lower** 더 낮은 **cave** 동굴
expect 예상하다

정답 : ④

[유형 6] 흐름과 관계없는 문장 고르기

21 다음 글에서 전체 흐름과 관련이 없는 문장은?

① Animals have magic power to help people. ② Scientists think the magic is simply love and trust. ③ People want to find some unusual animals. ④ Pets usually welcome people and show them love.

words

magic 신비로운, 불가사의한 (힘), 마술 **scientist** 과학자
simply 그저, 단순히 **trust** 신뢰 **unusual** 특이한, 드문
welcome 다정하게 맞이하다, 환영하다

정답 : ③

22 다음 글에서 전체 흐름과 관련이 없는 문장은?

① When you apply for a job, you need to think about the personal happiness it could bring. ② You need to decide if this is the kind of job you would like to do. ③ Doctors can make much money. ④ Think about how you would enjoy working at this job day after day.

words

apply for ~에 지원하다 **personal** 개인적인 **happiness** 행복
decide 결정하다 **day after day** 매일같이, 날마다

정답 : ③

23 다음 글에서 전체 흐름과 관련이 없는 문장은?

Teens who cannot stop using computers by themselves show various symptoms. ① They become upset when not using computers. ② Some stay up all night to use computers. ③ You should protect animals. ④ These symptoms can be harmful to teens' health.

words

by oneself 혼자서	**various** 다양한	**symptom** 증상, 증세
upset 화난, 속상한	**stay up** 자지 않고 깨어 있다	**all night** 밤새도록
protect 보호하다		

정답 : ③

24 다음 글의 전체 흐름과 가장 관계가 없는 문장은?

Traveling gives you new pleasure of experiencing new things around the world. ① This world has many things that you haven't seen before. ② I will go shopping next weekend with my father. ③ However, traveling might not always be enjoyable unless you prepare for it. ④ Therefore, you should make plans for traveling.

words

traveling 여행(하기)	**pleasure** 즐거움, 기쁨	**experience** 경험(하다)
around the world 세계적으로	**enjoyable** 즐거운	**unless** 만약 ~ 아니라면
prepare for ~을 준비하다	**therefore** 그러므로, 따라서	

정답 : ②

[유형 7] 주어진 글에 이어질 내용 찾기

25 다음 글에 이어질 내용으로 알맞은 것은?

Soccer is one of the most popular sports in the world. It is played by people of all ages in more than 200 countries. Do you know the origin of this popular game?

① 축구의 기원
② 축구의 규칙
③ 축구의 인기도
④ 축구 인구의 증가

words

popular 인기 있는, 대중적인
age 나이
origin 기원, 유래

정답 : ①

26 다음 글에 이어질 내용으로 알맞은 것은?

The earth is our home and we must share the earth with all its plants and animals. But our earth is being polluted by us ever day. Can you think of some things you can do to protect the earth?

① 지구의 생성 과정
② 지구의 동물과 식물
③ 지구 오염의 종류
④ 지구를 보호하는 방법

words

earth 지구
share A with B A를 B와 공유하다, 나누다
pollute 오염시키다
protect 보호하다

정답 : ④

27 다음 글 바로 뒤에 올 내용으로 가장 알맞은 것은?

Every day, more than 28 million people around the world use the Internet. However, even with the many useful functions of the Net, some experts warn of the danger of Internet Addiction Disorder.

① 인터넷의 유용성
② 인터넷 예절의 중요성
③ 인터넷 사용 인구
④ 인터넷 중독의 위험성

words

million 백만
even 심지어 ~조차도
useful 유용한
function 기능, 역할
expert 전문가
warn 경고하다
danger 위험
addiction 중독
disorder 장애, ~증

정답 : ④

28 다음 글 바로 뒤에 이어질 내용으로 가장 알맞은 것은?

Today, tomatoes are one of the most common foods in the world. They are served alone or with your favorite dishes such as pizza and spaghetti. Here are some various recipes for tomatoes.

① 토마토의 가격
② 토마토의 요리법
③ 토마토의 생산지
④ 토마토의 재배 방법

words

common 흔한, 보통의
food 식품, 음식
serve 제공하다
alone 혼자, 단독으로
favorite 마음에 드는, 가장 좋아하는
dish 요리, 음식, 접시
recipe 요리법

정답 : ②

[유형 8] 주어진 문장 삽입하기

29 다음 문장이 들어가기에 가장 알맞은 곳은?

After we finished putting up the tent, we cooked lunch.

My friends and I went camping at a mountain last weekend. (①) Arriving there, we started to put up our tent. (②) While we were cooking, many insects gathered around us. (③) They bit and made us mad. (④)

words

put up 세우다, 설치하다 **insect** 곤충, 벌레 **gather** 모이다
bite-bit-bitten 물다 **mad** 미친, 몹시 화난

정답 : ②

30 다음 문장이 들어가기에 가장 알맞은 곳은?

As I had a few hours to spend until then, I decided to watch a movie.

One morning, my father asked me to drive him into town. (①) When we arrived, I promised to pick him up at 4 p.m. (②) I was enjoying the movie so much and I completely forgot about the time. (③) When the movie had finished, I was two hours late! (④)

words

spend (시간을) 보내다 **decide** 결심(결정)하다 **pick up** ~를 차로 태우러 가다
completely 완전히 **forget** 잊다

정답 : ②

31 다음 문장이 들어가기에 가장 알맞은 곳은?

But one woman changed this idea.

Today, anyone can learn to fly airplanes. (①) But this was not true in 1903. (②) At that time, people thought only men could be pilots. (③) Her name was Amelia Earhart. (④)

words

fly 날다, 조종하다
true 사실의, 진실한
pilot 조종사

정답 : ③

32 다음 문장이 들어가기에 가장 알맞은 곳은?

Instead I decided to make them with paper myself.

On the way home, I wanted to buy carnations for my parents. (①) I went to a flower shop. (②) However, I gave up buying them because of their high price. (③) Fortunately, my parents really loved my carnations. (④)

words

instead 대신에
give up 포기(단념)하다
fortunately 다행스럽게도

정답 : ③

[유형 9] 내용 파악하기

33 담배를 끊을 때 사용할 수 있는 방법으로 언급되지 않은 것은?

If you want to quit smoking, you can. A good way to quit smoking is to exercise, drink more water and eat food with vitamins. Remember, the longer you wait to quit, the harder it will be.

① 운동하기 ② 물 마시기
③ 휴식 취하기 ④ 비타민 섭취하기

words

quit 끊다, 그만두다 **exercise** 운동하다
the 비교급 ~, the 비교급 … ~하면 할수록 더욱 더 …하다

정답 : ③

34 Interact 클럽의 주요 활동이 아닌 것은?

I am in a school club called 'Interact'. It mainly helps others and does good things for communities. These are the activities we did last year. We cleaned neighborhoods and helped old people.

① 등산하기 ② 다른 사람 돕기
③ 동네 청소하기 ④ 지역사회에 기여하기

words

mainly 주로 **community** 지역사회 **activity** 활동
neighborhood 이웃, 근처

정답 : ①

35 다음 글에서 설명하는 숲의 기능은?

Trees push their roots deep into the soil. Even when there are storms, the roots hold the soil in place. Without trees, the soil is washed away by the rainwater.

① 공기 정화 ② 병충해 예방
③ 토양 침식 방지 ④ 휴식 장소 제공

words

root 뿌리	**soil** 토양, 흙
in place 그(제) 자리에	**wash away** 씻어내다

정답 : ③

36 밑줄 친 two basic things가 가리키는 것으로 알맞은 것은?

Driving can be fun. However, most of drivers ignore two basic things when they drive: They forget to keep enough distance from the car in front, and they don't wear seat belts.

① 차선 지키기, 신호 지키기 ② 안전거리 확보, 차선 지키기
③ 안전거리 확보, 좌석벨트 착용 ④ 좌석벨트 착용, 규정 속도 유지

words

most of 대부분의	**ignore** 무시하다	**basic** 기본(기초)적인
distance 거리	**in front** 앞에	**wear** 착용하다
seat belt 좌석벨트		

정답 : ③

[유형 10] 지칭 추론하기

37 밑줄 친 This(this)가 가리키는 것은?

> This tells about the things they did, the food they ate, the people they met and how they felt during that day. Most people feel that keeping this is a very private thing. They don't like to show this to others.

① a pet
② a diary
③ a wallet
④ a mirror

words

during ~동안(내내)
keep a diary 일기를 쓰다
private 개인적인, 사적인
wallet 지갑

정답 : ②

38 밑줄 친 They가 가리키는 것은?

> They are very smart animals. They have four long legs and two big ears. They pull the cart and people ride on them. They eat carrots. They are cousins of horses.

① dogs
② rabbits
③ monkeys
④ donkeys

words

smart 영리한
cart 수레, 마차
ride (올라)타다
carrot 당근
cousin 사촌
donkey 당나귀

정답 : ④

39 밑줄 친 this가 가리키는 것은?

> In recent years, this has become very important. By using this you can find information on any subject and communicate with others anywhere in the world. Truly, this is making the world a global society.

① X-ray ② package
③ Internet ④ vacation

words

recent 최근	**information** 정보	**subject** 주제
communicate 소통(통신, 대화)하다	**anywhere** 어느 곳이든	**truly** 정말로, 진정으로
global 세계적인	**package** 소포, 포장	**vacation** 방학, 휴가

정답 : ③

40 밑줄 친 It(it)이 가리키는 것으로 알맞은 것은?

> It surrounds the earth. we cannot see, smell, or taste it. When the wind blows, you feel it against your face. All living things need it to stay alive.

① air ② soil
③ tree ④ water

words

surround 둘러싸다	**smell** 냄새를 맡다	**taste** 맛보다
blow (바람이) 불다	**against** ~에 부딪히는	**living thing** 생물, 생명체
alive 살아있는		

정답 : ①

[유형 11] 속담, 교훈

41 다음 격언이 주는 교훈으로 가장 알맞은 것은?

No pains, no gains.

① 노력 ② 관용
③ 감사 ④ 청결

정답 : ①

42 다음 격언이 주는 교훈으로 가장 알맞은 것은?

Honesty is the best policy.

① 정직 ② 인내
③ 협동 ④ 효도

정답 : ①

43 다음 밑줄 친 속담의 뜻은?

A : I'll ride my bike to school for my health and saving money.
B : It is to kill two birds with one stone.

① 모든 일에 조심해야 한다.
② 기회는 올 때 잡아야 한다.
③ 한 번에 두 가지 이득을 얻는다.
④ 부지런하면 언젠가 보상이 온다.

정답 : ③

44 다음 격언이 주는 교훈으로 가장 알맞은 것은?

Slow and steady wins the race.

① 성실 ② 우정
③ 신속 ④ 협동

정답 : ①

45 대화에서 밑줄 친 표현의 의미로 알맞은 것은?

A : Our team lost the soccer game. I don't know what to do.
B : I think that <u>practice makes perfect</u>.

① 행운을 기다려라.
② 꾸준히 연습하라.
③ 규칙을 잘 지켜라.
④ 협동심을 길러라.

정답 : ②

46 밑줄 친 격언이 주는 교훈으로 가장 알맞은 것은?

A : Good morning! You've come to work first again.
B : <u>The early bird catches the worm</u>.

① 용기 ② 협동
③ 배려 ④ 근면

정답 : ④

[유형 12] 실용문 - 게시문, 광고, 도표

47 다음 광고에서 알 수 없는 것은?

> ***Insa Art Gallery***
>
> Location : Insa-dong
>
> What to see : Old paintings, crafts, etc.
>
> Open : 10 a.m. ~ 9 p.m. Admission fee : Free

① 연락처 ② 입장료

③ 전시 내용 ④ 관람 시간

words

gallery 미술관, 화랑 **location** 위치 **craft** (수)공예
etc 기타 등등 **admission fee** 입장료

정답 : ①

48 다음 구인광고에서 알 수 없는 것은?

> **Wanted**
>
> • Position : Salesperson
> • Working Hours : 17:00~22:00
> • Pay : $5 / hour
> • Tel : 789-1234
>
> *Great Bookstore*

① 연락처

② 근무 요일

③ 근무 시간

④ 시간당 급여

words

wanted 구인광고 **position** 일자리, 직위
salesperson 판매원

정답 : ②

49 다음 축제 포스터에서 알 수 <u>없는</u> 것은?

① 기간
② 입장료
③ 장소
④ 상금

words

festival 축제
admission fee 입장료

정답 : ④

50 다음 라벨에서 언급되지 <u>않은</u> 것은?

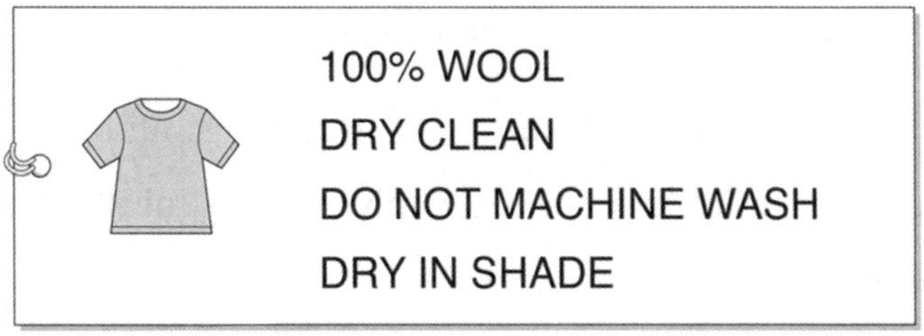

① 옷의 소재
② 세탁 방법
③ 건조 방법
④ 착용 방법

words

wool 양모, 울
machine wash 세탁기로 세탁하다
shade 그늘, 응달

정답 : ④

51 도표를 보고 빈칸에 들어갈 말로 알맞은 것을 고르시오.

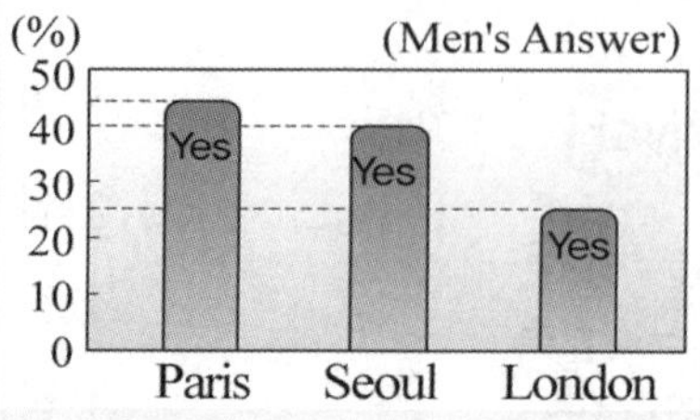

The percentage of people who cook meal is 15 percent ________ in London than in Seoul.

① more ② lower ③ better ④ higher

words

percentage(=percent) 백분율, 비율
meal 식사

정답 : ②

52 도표를 보고 빈칸에 들어갈 말로 알맞은 것을 고르시오.

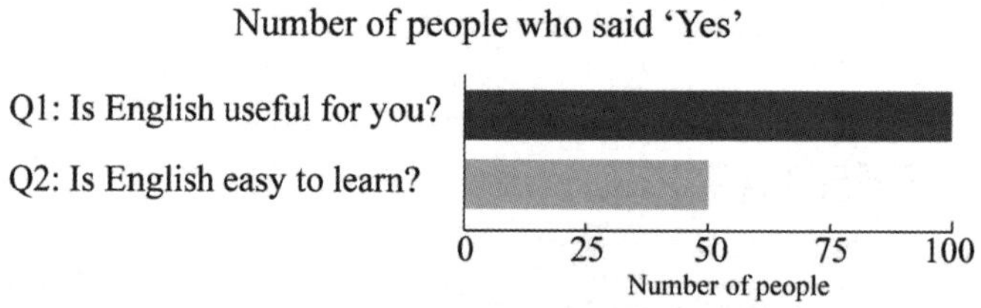

We asked one hundred people the above two questions. All of the people answered that English is useful for them. Still only ________ of them said that English is easy to learn.

① a half ② one-third
③ a quarter ④ one-fifth

words

useful 유용한	**above** 위의	**still** 그런데도
a half 1/2	**one-third** 1/3	**a quarter** 1/4
one-fifth 1/5		

정답 : ①

53 도표의 내용으로 보아 빈칸에 들어갈 말로 알맞은 것은?

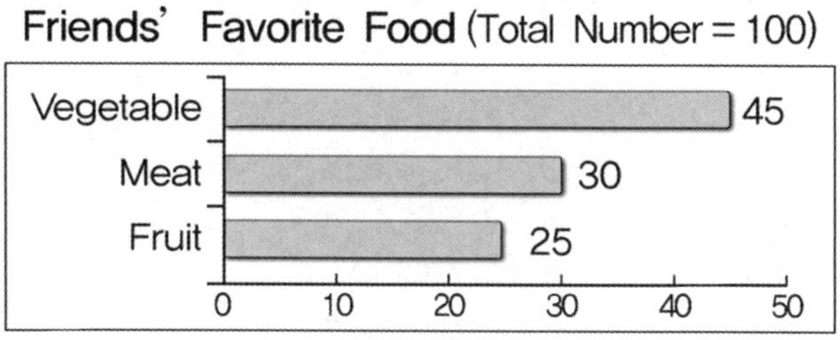

We asked one hundred friends about their favorite food. It show that just ______ of them like fruit.

① a half
② a third
③ a quarter
④ a fifth

words

favorite (가장) 좋아하는
vegetable 채소
meat 고기
fruit 과일

정답 : ③

54 도표의 내용으로 보아 빈칸에 들어갈 말로 알맞은 것은?

Our Students' Favorite Free-time Activities

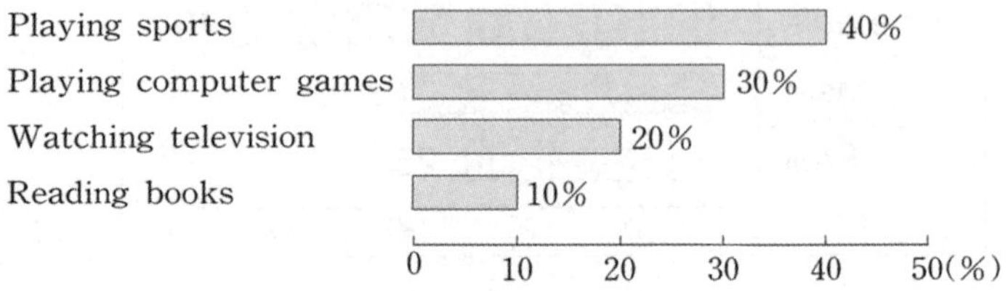

> The above graph shows what our students do in their free time. ________ is the most favorite activity of our students.

① Playing sports
② Playing computer games
③ Watching television
④ Reading books

words

graph 그래프 **free time** 자유 시간
activity 활동

정답 : ①

[유형 13] 장문 독해

[55~56] 다음 글을 읽고 물음에 답하시오.

Trees not only make life possible, but also make the air clean. Humans and animals breathe in oxygen and breathe out carbon dioxide. Trees do the opposite. In this way they help to keep the air clean and fresh. ____________, trees soak up water from the soil, which helps to prevent floods during heavy rain.

55 윗글의 주제로 가장 알맞은 것은?

① 홍수 예방 시기
② 토양 관리 방법
③ 공기청정기 원리
④ 나무가 주는 혜택

56 윗글의 흐름으로 보아 빈칸에 들어갈 말로 알맞은 것은?

① But
② Instead
③ In addition
④ For example

words

not only A but also B A뿐만 아니라 B도 역시		**possible** 가능한
oxygen 산소	**breathe in** 숨을 들이쉬다	**breathe out** 숨을 내쉬다
carbon dioxide 이산화탄소	**the opposite** 정반대	**soak up** 흡수하다
soil 토양	**prevent** 예방하다	**flood** 홍수
instead 대신에	**in addition** 게다가, 더욱이	**for example** 예를 들어

정답 : 55. ④ 56. ③

[57~58] 다음 글을 읽고 물음에 답하시오.

Nearly 50% of all workers have jobs that they aren't happy with. Don't let this happen to you! If you want to find the right job, don't rush to look through the ads in the newspaper. ___________, sit down and think about yourself. What kind of person are you? What makes you happy?

57 윗글의 주제로 가장 알맞은 것은?

① 올바른 직업 찾기
② 실직 문제의 심각성
③ 신문 광고의 효과
④ 근로자의 여가 활용

58 윗글의 흐름으로 보아 빈칸에 들어갈 말로 알맞은 것은?

① Instead
② Besides
③ Therefore
④ For instance

words

nearly 거의
rush 급히 가다, ~을 서두르다
look through ~을 훑어보다
therefore 그러므로
happen 일어나다
besides 게다가
ads(= advertisements) 광고
for instance 예를 들어

정답 : 57. ① 58. ①

[59~60] 다음 글을 읽고 물음에 답하시오.

Each culture has its own customs. They are not "right" or "wrong," but just different. ________________, when we meet foreigners, we should be careful not to judge their actions in our own way. Rather, we should learn to understand other culture with open mind.

59 윗글의 흐름으로 보아 빈칸에 들어갈 말로 알맞은 것은?

① Therefore
② However
③ In contrast
④ On the other hand

60 윗글의 요지로 가장 알맞은 것은?

① 우리 문화의 우수성을 알리자.
② 문화 예술에 대한 투자를 늘리자.
③ 문화 차이를 이해하고 받아들이자.
④ 후손을 위해 우리 문화재를 잘 보존하자.

words

culture 문화
own 자신만의
custom 풍습, 관습
not A but B A가 아니라 B
foreigner 외국인
careful 신중한, 주의 깊은
judge 판단하다
action 행동, 동작
rather 오히려
understand 이해하다
therefore 그러므로
however 하지만
in contrast 그에 반해서
on the other hand 다른 한 편으로는, 반면에

정답 : 59. ① 60. ③

※ [1~2] 다음 글의 흐름으로 보아, 빈칸에 들어갈 말로 알맞은 것을 고르시오.

1. Too much snow in one place can cause a lot of harm to the land, to people, and to buildings. In general, ________, snow is quite helpful. A good covering of snow on a farmer's field helps keep plants alive. Air under the snow is much warmer than air above it.

① besides ② for example
③ therefore ④ however

2. There are now more and more cars on the roads. But some drivers don't pay attention to their driving: They drive too fast or think about other things while driving. As a result, car accidents take place very often. So, we must be very ________ on the roads.

① fast ② kind
③ careful ④ careless

3. 다음 글에 나타난 'I'의 심정은?

At sixteen, I was at school. At thirty-two, I'm still at school. But, this time, I am at school as a teacher, not a student. When I was a student, the people I respected were teachers, neither lawyers nor doctors. I like to teach my students. They also like to learn from me.

① happy ② tired
③ painful ④ afraid

4. 다음은 두 학생의 여가 활용에 관한 도표이다. 내용과 <u>다른</u> 것은?

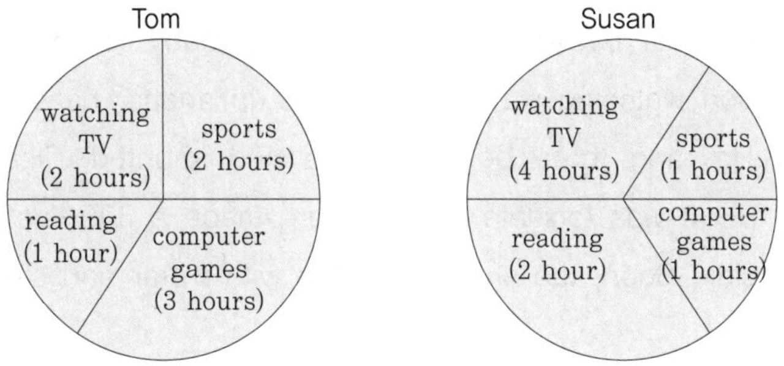

① Susan likes watching TV best.
② Susan spends less time on reading than Tom.
③ Tom likes playing computer games best.
④ Tom spends more time on sports than Susan.

5. 다음 글의 전체 내용으로 보아, 밑줄 친 부분의 의미로 알맞은 것은?

> Like many sisters, Eliza and Abby <u>couldn't be more different</u>. Twelve-year-old Eliza always has something to say and likes to play with a ball. On the other hand, nine-year-old Abby is always quiet and feels happiest with a good book to read.

① 성격이 매우 닮았다.
② 성격이 매우 다르다.
③ 외모가 매우 닮았다.
④ 외모가 매우 다르다.

6. 다음 글에서 느껴지는 분위기는?

> At that time, most passengers were getting ready for bed. Out in the cold, a man stood watching waves. Suddenly, up ahead, he saw something in the water. He rang three bells at once and shouted, "Iceberg! Right ahead! Stop!" But it was too late. The iceberg made a 300-foot hole in the Titanic's right side. Soon, the ship was filling with water and sinking fast.

① romantic ② boring
③ pleasant ④ urgent

7. 다음 글의 주제는?

> When I was a child, there was a river in front of my house. It was very clean. I used to swim and catch fish there. Sometimes my mother used to wash clothes in the river. But, now the river is not as clean as before. It is much polluted by garbage. So I can't go there any more for swimming or fishing.

① 수질 오염 ② 여가 선용
③ 고향 생각 ④ 쓰레기 재활용

8. 다음 글에서 전체 흐름과 관계가 없는 문장은?

> Early kites were used for many purposes. ① In Korea, people used to fly kites before the end of a year in order to take away bad luck. ② Kites were also used for sending messages. ③ Kites were made of silk and bamboo a long time ago. ④ Sometimes people used kites for warning of danger in real battles. And some kites were used for sport fighting.

9. 다음 글에 나타난 Frank에 관한 설명으로 일치하지 않는 것은?

> Frank is now the head of a very large company, but as a boy he used to work in a small shop. At that time he repaired bicycles and worked fourteen hours a day. He saved money for years and in 1938 he bought a small factory of his own. During the war Frank made spare parts for airplanes. By the end of the war, his small factory had become a large one.

① 어렸을 때는 작은 가게에서 일했다.
② 하루에 14시간 자전거 고치는 일을 했다.
③ 돈을 모아 1938년에 작은 공장을 샀다.
④ 전쟁 중에는 자동차 부품을 만들었다.

10. 다음 글에서 말하고자 하는 내용으로 가장 적절한 것은?

> When you are young, you don't have to be afraid of making mistakes in trying to find your own goal. It is like learning to play a game, like baseball or basketball. You can hardly expect to learn without making good many mistakes in the process.

① 규칙적인 생활을 해라.
② 실패를 두려워하지 말라.
③ 남의 말에 귀를 기울여라.
④ 성취 가능한 목표를 세워라.

※ [11~12] 다음 글의 흐름으로 보아 빈칸에 들어갈 말로 가장 적절한 것을 고르시오.

11.

Sharks live in every ocean in the world, but most sharks live in warm water. Sometimes they help to keep the oceans ________ because they eat sick fish, sick animals, and so on.

① calm
② dark
③ clean
④ dirty

12.

Our country has a long history. It has experienced many wars. In the past, Korea was poor and depended on foreign countries. Now Korea itself, ____________, can help poor countries since it has developed so much socially and economically.

① however
② moreover
③ therefore
④ besides

13. 다음 글의 내용으로 보아 밑줄 친 something이 가리키는 것은?

Jane and Dad were making something. They did not tell Mom what they were doing. They used paper and bamboo sticks. They worked for a long time. After lunch, Jane said to Mom, "Come to the park with us. We have a surprise for you." They all went to the park. The surprise was a beautiful kite. It went high up in the sky.

① 활 ② 연 ③ 윷 ④ 팽이

14. 다음 글의 요지로 가장 알맞은 것은?

> What kind of food do you like to eat? Many people prefer to eat food from their own culture. Some people dislike certain food because they are not used to it. The Japanese enjoy eating raw horse meat, but few Americans would want to taste it. Many Asians don't like pizza, which is a very popular food in the United States.
>
> * raw : 날것의

① 일본인은 생식을 즐긴다.
② 음식을 가려서는 안 된다.
③ 피자는 세계적인 음식이다.
④ 문화에 따라 선호하는 음식이 다르다.

15. 다음 글의 흐름으로 보아 어울리지 <u>않는</u> 것을 고르시오.

> Before you leave home, think carefully about what you will wear on the flight. Choose comfortable clothing that is not tight. ① Wear comfortable shoes because your feet will get bigger during the flight. ② If your shoes are tight, they will be uncomfortable. ③ Choose books which you can read. ④ You can take slippers to wear on the plane.

16. 다음 글의 제목으로 가장 알맞은 것은?

> The computer mouse was invented in 1964. The first mouse was made of wood, and had just one button. The first mouse was used in 1984. Nowadays almost every computer has a mouse. You use your mouse to move your cursor on the desktop. Though the mouse was invented in the 1964, it took about 20 years for the mouse to become popular.
>
> * desktop 데스크톱 (컴퓨터 작동 후의 기본화면)

① The Origin of a Computer Mouse
② The History of a Computer
③ The kind of a Computer Mouse
④ The Function of a Computer

17. 다음 글의 바로 뒤에 이어질 내용으로 가장 알맞은 것은?

Some people learn a new language easily. Other people have trouble learning a new language. How can you help yourself learn a foreign language, such as English? There are several ways to make learning English a little easier and more interesting.

① 영어의 중요성
② 영어가 어려운 이유
③ 영어를 공부하는 목적
④ 영어를 쉽게 배우는 방법

18. 다음 글의 밑줄 친 They가 가리키는 대상으로 가장 적절한 것은?

They were built as tombs for Egyptian kings and queens. They are made of huge stones. Usually, there is a room where the dead Pharaoh is kept. The Egyptians believed that there was an afterlife. They were designed to provide kings with everything they would need to make a journey to another life.

① 공원
② 왕궁
③ 피라미드
④ 박물관

19. 다음 글의 요지로 가장 적절한 것은?

Last Sunday, I went to the park near my house to enjoy the sun. There were many people who made a lot of noise. Some young people played loud music and danced. Some dogs barked loudly, but the owners didn't stop them. The park was so noisy that I couldn't rest. In my opinion, we should think about others in public places.

① 공공장소에 개를 데려오지 말자.
② 공공장소에서 남을 배려하자.
③ 공원에서 춤을 추지 말자.
④ 공원에서 햇빛을 즐기자.

20. 주어진 문장이 들어가기에 가장 적절한 곳은?

Later, humans began to learn how to control nature.

Nature existed long before humans. The first humans lived in a natural way. (①) They gathered fruits, berries, and roots to eat. (②) They did not cut stones into tools. (③) They did not change nature. (④) They made tools to plant food and they made weapons to hunt animals.

21. 다음 글의 내용을 가장 적절하게 표현한 속담은?

There was a boy whose hands were black with shoe polish. But his eyes shone with hope. He tried to smile even in difficult times. People asked him if he liked shining shoes. He said, "Sure, I'm brushing up on hope." This boy later became a great movie star and producer, Charlie Chaplin, who made Modern Times and The Kid.

① Where there is a will, there is a way.
② Two heads are better than one.
③ A friend in need is a friend indeed.
④ Don't cry over spilt milk.

22. 다음 글의 내용을 한 문장으로 요약하고자 한다. 빈칸에 가장 적절한 말은?

Dreams are always very good to have. But in order to achieve your dream, you should work hard. To be a dancer, make it a rule to practice dancing every day. Rome was not built in a day.

↓

Work hard, and your dream will ______________.

① come true
② rise
③ put off
④ fall

※ [23~24] 다음 글의 흐름으로 보아 빈칸에 들어갈 말로 가장 적절한 것을 고르시오.

23.

A person, a place, a thing, or an event has its own meaning and stands for something beyond itself as well. Examples of ________ are all around us in music, on television, and in everyday conversation. The dove represents peace, and the red rose stands for true love.

① facts
② symbols
③ ideas
④ themes

24.

Human memory does not work like a video camera. It is actually weak in many ways. During every stage of memory process, it is possible for people to __________. For example, about 4,000 people each year in the U.S. are arrested because of wrong witnesses. They may create people or events that their eyes did not see.

* witness 목격자

① work hard
② prepare events
③ make errors
④ get information

25. 다음 글에 나타난 필자의 주장으로 가장 적절한 것은?

As the population of the world increases, countries need to produce more food. How can we solve this problem? One way to increase the food supply is for people to start eating different plants. There are 20,000 kinds of plants for humans to eat. We, therefore, should find the ways to grow and eat some of those plants.

① 식용 가능한 식물을 찾아서 재배해야 한다.
② 곡물 재배를 위한 장소를 확보해야 한다.
③ 인구 증가를 낮출 방안을 찾아야 한다.
④ 곡물의 질병을 막는 기술을 개발해야 한다.

26. 다음은 Hemingway에 대한 설명이다. 내용과 일치하지 <u>않는</u> 것은?

> Earnest Hemingway was born in Oak Park, Illinois. But he spent 17 years in northern Michigan, where his father introduced him to hunting and fishing. In high school, Hemingway played boxing and American football. When the United States entered World War I, he volunteered and became an American ambulance driver in Italy. After returning from the war, he wrote many novels about war.

① Illinois 주에서 태어났다.
② 아버지로부터 낚시를 배웠다.
③ 고교 시절에 미식축구를 했다.
④ 의사로서 전쟁에 자원했다.

27. 주어진 문장에 이어질 글의 순서로 가장 적절한 것은?

> Japanese are considered to be one of the healthiest people in the world.

> (A) According to these doctors, three of the most important factors are diet, exercise, and lifestyle.
> (B) Many doctors have tried to find out the reason why Japanese can enjoy such advantages.
> (C) For example, their rates of heart disease and cancer are far lower than those in other countries.

① (A) – (B) – (C)　　② (A) – (C) – (B)
③ (C) – (A) – (B)　　④ (C) – (B) – (A)

28. 다음 글의 내용을 한 문장으로 요약하고자 한다. 빈칸에 가장 적절한 것은?

E-mail has become the basic means of communication in the Information Age. However, e-mail may soon be useless as people are becoming blocked on spam mail. Choosing a long e-mail name is a good way to prevent you from receiving spam mail. Use a mix of letters and numbers. This decreases the chance that the spam mail programs find your e-mail.

↓

Using a long e-mail name is a good way to _____ receiving spam mail.

① find
② avoid
③ click
④ increase

29. Honeybee에 관한 다음 글의 내용과 일치하지 <u>않는</u> 것은?

The honeybee, like all insects, has a body that is divided into three parts. It has five eyes: three small ones that form a triangle on top of its head and a large eye on each side of its head. The bee has three legs on each side of its chest. It uses its legs for walking and for brushing flower powder off its body. The bee uses its tongue to drink water and honey.

① 몸이 세 부분으로 구분된다.
② 다섯 개의 눈이 크기가 같다.
③ 가슴에 여섯 개의 다리가 있다.
④ 다리로 몸에 붙은 꽃가루를 털어 낸다.

30. 다음 글의 빈칸에 들어갈 말로 가장 적절한 것을 고르면?

How do stripes protect a zebra? You might think that in Africa the black-and-white zebra stands out from the crowd, making it an easy target for a passing lion. _________, the zebra's stripes actually help the animal hide in the open area. From a distance, a group of zebras look like waves of black and white lines, confusing a hungry lion. The lion can't pick out a single animal to attack. The lion moves away and the zebras' lives are saved.

① Thus
② Similarly
③ However
④ In addition

실전모의고사
1, 2회 풀어보기

01 실전모의고사

※ [1~3] 밑줄 친 부분의 뜻으로 알맞은 것을 고르시오.

1. You should put more effort into your work.

① 효과　② 노력　③ 인내　④ 애정

2. Please, keep in mind what I said.

① forget　② remove　③ fill　④ remember

3. I am ashamed of myself for making too many mistakes.

① 부끄럽다　② 자랑스럽다
③ 반대하다　④ 광고하다

4. 다음 중 두 단어의 의미 관계가 나머지 셋과 다른 것은?

① wide – narrow　② deep – shallow
③ lazy – idle　④ high – low

5. 다음 안내문의 내용과 일치하는 것은?

Instructions

- For fevers and headaches
- Two pills should be taken after each meal
- To be taken with a glass of water
- Not for children seven years and under
- To be kept out of the reach of children

① 열이 있을 때 복용해서는 안 된다.
② 식사하기 전에 두 알을 복용한다.
③ 우유와 함께 복용한다.
④ 아이의 손이 닿지 않는 곳에 보관한다.

※ [6~8] 빈칸에 공통으로 들어갈 말로 알맞은 것을 고르시오.

6.

· Finally, you have to be ________.
· The ________ is much better today.

① courage
② patient
③ belief
④ present

7.

· There is a grocery ________ across the street.
· They ________ the sun's light to power the plane.

① part
② food
③ store
④ fly

8.

· You may go to the concert, ______ you want to.
· He asked me ______ I knew Chinese.

① if
② though
③ as
④ whether

9. 다음 대화에서 밑줄 친 격언의 의미로 알맞은 것은?

A : My mother often says, "<u>Don't judge a book by its cover</u>."
B : What does that mean?

① 계획보다 실천이 중요하다.
② 매사에 자신감을 느끼고 행동하라.
③ 겉만 보고 속을 판단하지 마라.
④ 책을 읽으면, 아는 만큼 보인다.

10. 다음 대화에서 알 수 있는 B의 심정으로 가장 알맞은 것은?

A : Did your interview go well?
B : I don't know. The result will come out today.
A : Really? I think you will hear good news today.
B : Do you think so? I can't stop worrying.
A : Don't worry. You're the right man for the job.

① delighted ② worried
③ excited ④ bored

11. 다음 대화가 이루어지는 장소로 가장 알맞은 것은?

A : How can I help you?
B : I lost my wallet. I came here to check if someone turn it in.
A : What does it look like?
B : It's red and there is a zipper on its side.
A : A red wallet? Oh, is this yours?

① a department store ② a bus stop
③ a restaurant ④ a lost & found office

※ [12~13] 대화의 빈칸에 들어갈 말로 가장 알맞은 것을 고르시오.

12.

A : Why don't you come with me?
B : ______________ I have a lot of work to do.

① I'd love to, but I can't. ② Sure, I'd love to.
③ Why not? ④ Okay, I will.

13.

A : Do you have the time?
B : ________________

① I'm sorry I don't have a watch.
② I'm sorry I'm busy now.
③ Yes, I'm free this evening.
④ Not today.

14. 주어진 말에 이어질 두 사람의 대화의 순서로 알맞은 것은?

Did you finish packing your bag?

(A) All right. You'd better go to sleep early.
(B) I packed almost everything.
(C) Yes, Mom. Could you wake me up at 7?

① (A) – (C) – (B)　　② (B) – (A) – (C)
③ (C) – (A) – (B)　　④ (C) – (B) – (A)

15. 다음 글에서 세 번째로 흔한 혈액형은?

Karl Landsteiner first thought of naming blood types in 1900. He divided blood into four types, such as A, B, AB, and O. Blood type O is the most common around the world. Blood type A is the second most common, and type AB is the least common of all types.

① A　　② O　　③ B　　④ AB

16. 다음 글을 쓴 목적으로 가장 알맞은 것은?

I live near an airport. Jets fly over my house day and night. Jets invade my privacy. I can't read. I can't watch TV, either. An old man lives next door to my house. He suffers from the noise, too. He is sick and in the hospital now.

① 감사 ② 충고 ③ 위로 ④ 불평

17. 밑줄 친 This(this)가 가리키는 것으로 알맞은 것은?

This can be sent to millions of email users with the click of a button. Sometimes this spread harmful viruses to lots of computers.

① blog ② hacker ③ spam ④ messenger

18. 다음 문장이 들어가기에 가장 알맞은 곳은?

Because of this, we should not shout into other person's ears.

There are some things we can do to protect our ears. (①) Loud noises may harm the ears. (②) Hitting the ear may harm it. (③) So, never hit anyone on the ear. (④) Be careful about pushing anything into the ear.

19. 다음 글의 제목으로 가장 알맞은 것은?

> There are many causes of hunger in Africa. African governments can't supply enough food for all their people because of rapid population growth. Secondly, long periods without rain often cause them to have little food. Also many civil wars and poor transportation are causes of hunger.
>
> * civil war 내전 * transportation 운송수단

① 아프리카 기아의 원인
② 다양한 아프리카 농작물
③ 아프리카의 인구변화
④ 운송수단의 현대화

※ [20~21] 다음 글의 빈칸에 들어갈 말로 가장 알맞은 것을 고르시오.

20.

> Many people worry about the loss of their memories, but experts say that forgetting something is normal. If we remember everything, we would have a lot of difficulties. Forgetting is as important as ________.

① brain
② thought
③ studying
④ memory

21.

> Watching a movie ________ can be very convenient, and a lot cheaper. People can stop the movie to make some snacks, answer the phone, or check on the baby. There are no lines to stand in, no tickets to buy.

① alone
② at home
③ for free
④ on weekends

22. 다음은 Cacao 나무에 관한 설명이다. 내용과 일치하지 않는 것은?

Chocolate comes from cacao trees. These trees grow well in countries with a tropical climate which is hot and wet. They are about six meters tall and have big green leaves. Chocolate is made from cacao beans which are the fruit of the tree. Cacao trees have their first fruit when they are three to four years old. Some cacao trees grow to be 200 years old, but most trees have fruit for about 25 years.

① 열대 기후에서 잘 자란다.
② 초콜릿의 원료는 cacao 열매이다.
③ 첫 열매는 심은 지 3~4년 만에 수확된다.
④ 평균 수명이 25년이다.

23. 다음 글의 흐름과 관계없는 문장은?

The water is warm when the sun shines on it. ① Some of this water goes up into the sky and makes clouds. ② The wind carries the clouds for hundreds of kilometers. ③ Then the clouds meet cold air in the sky, and we see drops of water. ④ So water is always moving from rivers to oceans. The drops of water are rain.

※ [24~25] 다음 글을 읽고 물음에 답하시오.

We know that regular exercises is good for us. However, most of us don't realize that we should do some stretching before exercising. There are many benefits you can get from stretching. Stretching makes your body more flexible and helps your body stay balanced. __________, it keeps your body in shape and prevents muscles from getting hurt. It can reduce stress as well.

* flexible 유연한

24. 윗글의 흐름으로 보아 빈칸에 알맞은 것은?

① In addition
② However
③ For example
④ Unfortunately

25. 윗글의 주제로 가장 적절한 것은?

① 스트레스 해소 방법
② 지나친 운동의 위험성
③ 스트레칭의 좋은 점
④ 운동의 다양한 종류

02 실전모의고사

※ [1~2] 밑줄 친 부분의 뜻으로 알맞은 것을 고르시오.

1. He was <u>satisfied</u> with the result.

① 초조한　② 우울한　③ 만족한　④ 염려하는

2. I could not <u>make out</u> what she said.

① 이해하다　② 기억하다　③ 암기하다　④ 듣다

3. 밑줄 친 부분과 의미가 같은 것은?

> The traffic accident <u>took place</u> near the bus stop.

① destroyed　② happened
③ polluted　④ removed

4. 두 단어의 관계가 나머지 셋과 <u>다른</u> 것은?

① wide – width　② deep – depth
③ long – length　④ grow – growth

※ [5~7] 다음 빈칸에 들어갈 말로 알맞은 것을 고르시오.

5.

> I heard my name ______ behind me.

① call　② to call　③ called　④ calling

6.

Do you know ____________________?

① how is it much
② how much it is
③ how much is it
④ how it is much

7.

In summer, some people go to the seaside, and __________ go to the mountain.

① others
② another
③ the other
④ one

8. 다음 대화의 빈칸에 들어갈 말로 적절하지 않은 것은?

A : What does he do for a living?
B : ____________________.

① He teaches Math
② He is a lawyer
③ He works for a bank
④ He does his homework

9. 다음 대화에서 두 사람의 관계로 알맞은 것은?

A : Let's go to the Dongdaemoon Stadium.
B : OK. Are you going to watch a game, ma'am?
A : No. I'm going there for shopping.
B : Oh, I see. Fasten your seat belt, please.

① teacher – student
② customer – clerk
③ passenger – taxi driver
④ mother – son

10. 다음 대화가 이루어지는 장소로 알맞은 것은?

A : Can I help you?
B : Yes. I'm looking for a pair of boots.
A : Sorry. We don't have any boots. How about sandals?
B : Sandals? OK! Do you have blue ones?

① In a bookstore ② In a clothes store
③ In a library ④ In a shoe store

11. 다음 대화에서 밑줄 친 부분의 의도로 알맞은 것은?

A : You know what? I got an F on my science test.
B : Oh, I'm sorry to hear that.
But Cheer up! I'm sure you will do better next time.

① 칭찬 ② 격려 ③ 감사 ④ 불평

12. 밑줄 친 I(me)가 가리키는 것은?

I am found in every country. People carry me with them when they go shopping. Most people have to work to get me. Buying and selling is done with me. I am made of copper, silver, or paper.

① Money ② A car ③ A basket ④ A market

13. 빈칸에 공통으로 들어갈 말로 가장 알맞은 것은?

________ control is important to your health. If you gain ________, you might have a heart attack. Therefore, you should control your _______.

① H(h)eight ② S(s)ize ③ H(h)abit ④ W(w)eight

14. 다음 글의 Mr. Pott의 성격으로 알맞은 것은?

> Mr. Pott will help anyone or anything in need. It could be a bird with a broken wing. Mr. Pott will know what to do to make it better. He'll take care of the bird, bring it food, and watch over it until the wing is cured.

① idle ② polite ③ kind ④ rude

※ [15~16] 글의 빈칸에 들어갈 말로 알맞은 것을 고르시오.

15.

> A mother or father is often a child's first reading teacher. By speaking a baby, parents help the baby understand what language is and what it is for. Children feel love in the sounds of words. They try to ________ back. As babies listen and speak, they store up facts and ideas.

① read ② talk ③ help ④ feel

16.

> Sand is found all over the world. Some sand is in the ground right around us. Much of it lies at the bottom of sea and lakes. It is rolled along the bottom of rivers and sometimes spreads over the river bank. Most ______ are dry places covered with sand.

① deserts ② mountains ③ oceans ④ roads

17. 다음에서 설명하는 것이 무엇인지 알맞은 것을 고르시오.

> They are animals without backbones. There are millions of different kinds. They are divided into three parts : the head, the middle part, and the hind part. They all have one pair of feelers and they all have six legs.

① insect ② fish ③ plant ④ bird

18. 주어진 문장 다음에 이어질 순서로 적절한 것은?

> Look at your hand. Many things have to happen so that you can see it. First, a picture of your hand is made in your eyes.

(A) These messages cause you to think about the picture.
(B) After all these things happen, you see your hand.
(C) Then, messages about the picture are sent from your eyes to your brain.

① (A) – (C) – (B)
② (C) – (A) – (B)
③ (C) – (B) – (A)
④ (A) – (B) – (C)

19. 다음 글의 주제로 가장 알맞은 것은?

> As the rain water moves, it picks up some salt from the ground and from rocks. The water takes the salt into rivers. Then the salty river water runs into the sea. River water has been running into the sea for a long, long time. So there is much salt in it.

① 빗물의 생성 과정
② 강의 생성 과정
③ 바닷물이 짠 이유
④ 소금이 짠 이유

20. 다음은 City Tour Bus 이용에 대한 안내문이다. 내용과 일치하지 <u>않는</u> 것은?

City Tour Bus

Adult ---------- $10
Student ---------- $ 8
Child(5-12 years) ---------- $ 5

♣ Children under 5 for free
♣ Group discounts available
♣ Tour takes about 1 hour
♣ Runs every 30 minutes, Friday to Sunday

① 단체 할인이 가능하다.
② 시내 관광에 1시간 정도 걸린다.
③ 버스는 30분마다 운행한다.
④ 매일 이용할 수 있다.

21. 다음 글의 목적으로 가장 알맞은 것은?

> The more often you make practical use of English, the faster you will learn it. It is useful to go on speaking and writing it constantly without being afraid of making mistakes.

① to appreciate
② to advise
③ to introduce
④ to praise

22. 다음 글에 이어질 내용으로 알맞은 것은?

> What kind of study habits do you have? Do you think your study habits are effective? Good study habits may save you some time and efforts. Here are some tips to help you develop good study habits.

① 좋은 공부 습관의 중요성
② 학습 시간 관리의 필요성
③ 좋은 공부 습관을 위한 비결
④ 공부 습관 교정의 어려움

23. 다음 글에서 전체 흐름과 관련이 <u>없는</u> 문장은?

> Here is a story about a man who made what many people wear today. His name was Levi Strauss. ① He started making and selling jeans in America in 19th century. ② Jeans sold well because they were just the right kind of clothing for workers. ③ They were very expensive for them. ④ Young people loved them, too. For the young, wearing jeans used to be a form of rebellion.
>
> * rebellion 반항

※ [24~25] 다음 글을 읽고 물음에 답하시오.

There once was a king who was defeated in a battle. While he was taking shelter in a cave from his enemy, he saw a spider. It was trying to make a spider web. As it climbed up, a thread in its web broke and it fell down. But it did not give up. It tried to climb again and again. ___________, the spider successfully completed the web. The king thought, "If a small spider can face failure so bravely, why should I give up?" Then, he collected his soldiers and fought against his enemy again and again. Finally, he regained his kingdom.

* spider web : 거미줄(집)

24. 윗글의 흐름으로 보아, 빈칸에 알맞지 않은 것은?

① At last
② Eventually
③ Finally
④ Occasionally

25. 윗글이 주는 교훈으로 가장 적절한 것은?

① 포기하지 않고 계속 도전해야 한다.
② 상대방의 처지에서 생각해야 한다.
③ 노력하는 자는 즐기는 자를 이길 수 없다.
④ 작은 일에도 감사하며 살아야 한다.

정답 및 해설

단원별확인문제

실전모의고사 1, 2

01. 어법(단원확인문제)

01. 명사와 대명사

1. ④	2. ②	3. ①	4. ④	
5. (1) ⓑ	(2) ⓒ	(3) ⓔ	(4) ⓐ	
6. ②	7. ①	8. ②	9. ②	10. ④

1. 단수를 나타낼 때는 a/an을 붙인다.

2. 차 한잔을 나타낼 때는 'a cup of tea' 라고 표현한다.

3. 단수를 나타내는 a가 나왔으므로 단수 명사를 이끈다.

4. 4형식 동사 gave 뒤에는 간접목적어, 직접목적어가 나와야 하며, 두 조각의 케이크를 표현할 때는 two pieces of를 쓴다.

5. (1) 세 장의 종이 : three sheets of paper
(2) 운동 이름은 무관사 play table tennis
(3) 한 켤레의 신발 : a pair of shoes
(4) 한 병의 물 : a bottle of water

6. 사람을 소개할 때는 this(이 분, 이 사람)라고 표현한다.

7. one은 앞에 나온 명사의 반복을 피하기 위해 쓰는데, 불특정한 대상을 나타낸다.
단수명사는 one으로 대신하고, 복수명사는 ones로 대신한다.
hat을 나타내는 one은 명사의 반복을 피하기 위해 사용되었으며 단수이므로 one을 쓴다.

8. one은 앞에 나온 명사의 반복을 피하기 위해 쓰는데, 불특정한 대상을 나타낸다.
단수명사는 one으로 대신하고, 복수명사는 ones로 대신한다.
drinks의 명사의 반복을 피하기 위해 복수로 ones를 쓴다.

9. 어떤 이들(some)은 ~, 다른 이들(others)은 …으로 표현한다.
어떤 이들은 야구를 좋아하고, 다른 이들은 야구를 좋아하지 않는다.

10. 두 개를 나타낼 때, 하나는 one, 다른 하나는 the other로 나타낸다.
두 권의 책이 있다. 한 권은 소설이고, 다른 한 권은 만화책이다.

02. 형용사와 부사

1. ③	2. ②	3. ①	4. ④	5. ②
6. ③	7. ④	8. ④	9. ②	10. ④

1. 돈은 셀 수 없으므로 명사를 꾸며주는 many가 올 수 없으며, much를 써야한다.

2. 뒤에 명사가 students가 왔으므로 셀 수 없는 명사를 꾸며주는 much가 올 수 없다.

3. flowers는 셀 수 있으므로 much가 올 수 없다. (many로 고쳐준다.)

4. hardly는 부정으로 '거의 ~않게' 를 의미하며 여기서는 열심히 일했다의 의미로 hard가 가능하다.

5. in, of가 오면 최상급을 쓰며 여기서는 Ann은 가장 나이가 어리므로 youngest를 쓴다.

6. 가장 키가 큰 사람은 John이다.

7. swim은 수영하다는 동사, swimmer는 수영하는 사람이라는 명사를 나타낸다.
나머지는 형용사와 비교급

8. in, of가 오면 최상급을 쓰며 최상급을 나타내는 표현은 best이다.

9. 두 명을 비교할 때는 비교급을 쓰며, 더 어리다는

표현은 younger이다.

10. 비교급-최상급-원급
메리는 앤보다 더 크다.
토미는 모두 중 가장 빠른 달리기 선수다.
이 비행기는 저 비행기보다 세 배 빨리 날 수 있다.

03. 문장의 형식

1. ②	2. ④	3. ④	4. ①	5. ②
6. ③	7. ①	8. ②	9. ④	10. ⓒ

1. 감각동사 뒤에는 부사가 올 수 없으며, 형용사만 가능하다.

2. 4형식 수여동사만 가능, said는 3형식 동사이므로 간접목적어, 직접목적어가 나올 수 없다.

3. 수여동사 teach는 뒤에 간접목적어, 직접목적어가 나온다.

4. made는 4형식에서 3형식으로 바뀔 때 전치사 for가 붙으며 나머지는 전치사 to가 나오는 동사들이다.

5. 감각동사 뒤에는 형용사만 가능하며, 부사는 올 수 없으므로 badly는 불가능하다.

6. want는 5형식 동사이며 to부정사를 목적격 보어로 취한다.

7. wrote는 4형식에서 3형식으로 바뀔 때 to, buy의 경우에는 for를 붙인다.

8. 감각동사 뒤에는 형용사만 가능하며 다른 품사는 불가능하다. sad만 올 수 있다.

9. ④는 4형식 수여동사로 쓰였으며 나머지는 5형식 일반동사로 목적격 보어 자리에 형용사가 왔다.

10. ask는 5형식 동사로 목적격 보어 자리에 to부정사만 가능하다.

04. 동사 시제

1. ④	2. ②	3. ③	4. ③	5. ③
6. ②	7. ③	8. ②	9. ③	10. ②

1. 일반적 사실을 나타내는 경우 현재 동사를 사용한다.
서울은 한국의 수도이다.

2. tomorrow라는 미래 시점이 나왔으므로 미래조동사 will을 쓴다.

3. last night이라는 명백한 과거 시점에는 과거동사만 가능하다.

4. twice와 함께 경험을 나타내는 현재완료로 쓰였다.
캐럴은 캐나다에 두 번 가본 경험이 있다.

5. 현재완료 계속적 용법으로 전치사 for와 함께 쓰였다. for 뒤에는 숫자와 함께와서 '동안'의 의미로 해석한다.

6. Was your sister~?로 물을 경우, 같은 주어 동사로 나와야 한다.

7. 불변의 법칙을 나타내는 경우 현재 동사를 사용한다.
지구는 태양 주변을 돈다.

8. 시간, 조건 부사절에서는 현재가 미래를 대신한다.

9. 시간, 조건 부사절에서는 현재가 미래를 대신한다.

10. 명백한 과거 시점에는 과거 동사만 가능하다.

05. 조동사

1. ①	2. ①	3. ④	4. ②	5. ⑤
6. ①	7. ②	8. ③	9. ④	10. ②

1. be able to = can 가능성을 나타낸다.
펭귄은 날 수 있니?

2. Can은 허락을 의미하며 may로 대신하여 쓸 수 있다.
마이크씨와 통화할 수 있을까요?

= 인수와 통화할 수 있을까요?

3. may는 약한 추측으로 쓰여 '~일지도 모른다'의 의미이지만 나머지는 전부 '해야한다'의 의미이다.

4. must have p.p : ~했음에 틀림없다.

5. shouldn't have p.p : ~하지 말았어야 했다. (후회)

6. may have p.p : ~했을지도 모른다. (약한 추측)

7. used to 동사원형 : ~하곤했다.

8. would rather A than B : B하느니 차라리 A하겠다.

9. don't have to : ~할 필요가 없다.
일부 학생들은 학교 교복을 입을 필요가 없다.

10. 나는 운전하지 말았어야했는데. (후회)

06. 준동사

1. ④	2. ③	3. ①	4. ②	5. ③
6. ①	7. ③	8. ③	9. ①	10. ②

1. 동명사 주어로 쓰여, crossing 길을 건너는 것으로 해석한다.
양쪽을 보지 않고 길을 건너는 것은 위험하다.

2. 형/부 enough to 동사원형 : ~할만큼 충분히 ~한
너는 그 자전거를 타기에 충분히 크다.

3. too ~ to : 너무 ~해서 ~할 수 없다.
그의 팔은 너무 짧아서 선반에 닿을 수 없었다.

4. be good at ~ing : ~을 잘하다. 능숙하다.
그는 영어 말하기를 잘한다.

5. can't help ~ing : ~하지 않을 수 없다. 그가 재밌는 이야기에 대해 말할 때 나는 웃지 않을 수 없다.

6. have difficulty ~ing : ~ing하는 데 어려움을 겪다.
내 친구는 쌍둥이를 구분하는 데 어려움을 겪는다.

7. 사물이 유발하는 상황이면 ing로, 지루함을 유발하므로 boring.
그 책을 읽는 것은 나에게 너무 지루하다.

8. 사람의 성격, 감정을 나타내는 경우 의미상 주어는 of.
be full of : ~로 가득차다.

9. 분사구문으로 바꿀 경우, 접속사 생략, 주절의 주어와 종속절의 주어가 같으면 주어 생략, 동사원형에 ing를 붙여준다.
앞에 접속사와 주어를 생략하며, watch에 ing를 붙여서 분사구문을 만든다.

10. 분사구문으로 바꿀 경우, 접속사 생략, 주절의 주어와 종속절의 주어가 같으면 주어 생략, 동사원형에 ing를 붙여준다.
앞에 접속사와 주어를 생략하며, be동사 원형에 ing를 붙여서 분사구문을 만든다.

07. 수동태

1. ④	2. ③	3. ④	4. to	5. in
6. at	7. with	8. ①	9. ③	10. ④

1. now 현재진행 시점과 주어와 동사가 수동의 의미를 가진다.
중요한 회의가 현재 회의실에서 개최되고 있는 중이다.

2. next week 미래 시점과 주어와 동사가 수동의 의미를 가진다.
새로운 제품이 다음 주에 출시될 것이다.

3. 명백한 과거 시점에서는 과거 동사만 나올 수 있다.
새로운 다리가 1950년에 지어졌다.

4. be known to : ~에게 알려지다.
그 가수는 많은 젊은이들에게 알려져있다.

5. be interested in : ~에 관심이 있다.
그녀는 춤추는 데 관심이 있니?

6. be surprised at : ~에 놀라다.
나의 엄마는 그 소음에 놀랐다

7. be filled with : ~로 가득 차다.
그의 사무실은 책으로 가득 차 있다.

8. be crowded with : ~로 가득 차 있다.
그 쇼핑몰은 사람들로 가득 차 있다

9. be interested in : ~에 관심이 있다.
나는 어렸을 때 스키 타는 데 관심이 있었다.

10. be made from : (화학적 변화) ~로 만들어지다.
치즈는 우유로 만들어진다.

08. 의문사와 관계사

1. who	2. that	3. what	4. ①
5. where	6. when	7. how	
8. ③	9. ①	10. ②	

1. 앞에 사람을 나타내는 선행사 an actor가 나왔으므로 who가 나온다.

2. 앞에 사물을 나타내는 선행사 a building이 나왔으므로 that이 나온다.

3. what은 '~하는 것'을 의미하며 선행사를 포함한 관계대명사이다.

4. the boy 사람을 나타내는 선행사이므로 who가 나온다.

5. 뒤에 완전한 절을 이끌며 장소를 나타내는 선행사가 나왔으므로 관계부사 where가 나온다.

6. 뒤에 완전한 절을 이끌며 시간을 나타내는 선행사가 나왔으므로 관계부사 when이 나온다.

7. the way와 how는 둘 중 하나만 쓸 수 있다.

8. 뒤에 완전한 절을 이끌며 장소를 나타내는 선행사가 나왔으므로 관계부사 where가 나온다.
우리가 이전에 만났던 장소는 미술관 앞이다.

9. 뒤에 완전한 절을 이끌며 시간을 나타내는 선행사가 나왔으므로 관계부사 when이 나온다.
너는 평창 올림픽이 언제였는지를 기억하니?

10. 뒤에 완전한 절을 이끌며 이유(the reason)를 나타내는 선행사가 나왔으므로 관계부사 why가 나온다.
나는 형편없는 성적을 받은 이유를 잘 모른다.

09. 가정법

1. ③	2. ②	3. would
4. would have passed		5. had had
6. ④	7. were	8. could
9. were	10. ②	

1. 가정법 과거에서 be동사는 무조건 were를 쓴다.
만일 내가 키가 크다면, 나는 더 자신감이 넘칠텐데.

2. 가정법 과거에서 be동사는 무조건 were를 쓴다.
만일 내가 건축가라면, 나는 나 자신의 집을 디자인할 텐데.

3. 가정법 과거로, would로 바꿔준다.
밖이 춥다. 만일 내가 너라면 나는 따뜻한 재킷을 입을 텐데.

4. 가정법 과거 완료로 would have p.p를 쓴다.

5. 가정법 과거 완료로 had p.p를 쓴다.

6. 첫 문장은 가정법 과거, 두 번째 문장은 가정법 과거완료이다.
만일 내가 너라면 나는 좀 쉴 텐데.
만일 마크가 전화를 했었더라면 나는 전화가 오는 소리를 들었을 텐데.

7. wish 가정법으로, 현재 시점과 함께 나와서 현재 사실과 반대를 나타내는 가정법과거 동사 were를 쓴다.

나는 현재 백만장자이길 소망한다.

8. wish 가정법으로, 과거 시점과 함께 나와서 과거 사실과 반대를 나타내는 가정법과거완료 동사 could have p.p를 쓴다.
나는 그 당시에 더 인내를 했었기를 소망한다.

9. 마치 ~라면 가정법 과거를 나타내는 were를 쓴다.
그는 마치 싱글인 것처럼 말한다. 하지만 그는 결혼을 했다.

10. wish 가정법으로, 가정법과거 동사를 쓴다.
나는 내가 학교 행사에 참여할 수 없어 유감이다.
→ 나는 학교 행사에 참여하기를 소망하다. (현재사실과 반대)

10. 접속사와 전치사

1. while	2. as	3. both	
4. unless	5. even if	6. ③	
7. ③	8. ①	9. ②	10. ③

1. while이 접속사이므로 뒤에 절이 온다.
너가 부산에 있는 동안 우리 집에 와.

2. as : ~할수록이라는 의미로 접속사 as가 문맥상 자연스럽다.
그가 나이가 들수록 더 현명해졌다.

3. both A and B : A와 B 둘 다
그 작가는 소설과 에세이 둘 다 쓴다.

4. unless : 만일 ~하지 않다면
날씨가 나쁘지 않다면 우리는 내일 캠핑에 갈 것이다.

5. even if : ~에도 불구하고
너는 이번에 실패했지만 또 다른 기회가 있을 것이다.

6. while은 접속사로서 절을 이끌며, '~동안'의 의미를 갖는다.
제임스는 내가 집을 청소하는 동안 설거지를 하고 있었다.

7. if : 만일 ~하면

8. although : 비록 ~일지라도

9. both A and B : A와 B 둘 다
김과 정 둘 다 시험 결과에 만족한다.

10. neither A nor B : A와 B 둘 다 아닌
데이빗과 브라이언 둘 다 달리기를 잘하지 못한다.

02. 생활영어(단원확인문제)

1. ①	2. ④	3. ②	4. ③	5. ①
6. ④	7. ③	8. ②	9. ④	10. ①
11. ③	12. ②	13. ②	14. ④	15. ③
16. ①	17. ①	18. ④	19. ②	20. ①
21. ②	22. ③	23. ③	24. ③	25. ④
26. ②	27. ①	28. ④	29. ③	30. ①
31. ④	32. ②	33. ①	34. ④	35. ①
36. ②	37. ③	38. ③	39. ②	40. ④
41. ④	42. ①	43. ④	44. ②	45. ②
46. ③	47. ①	48. ③	49. ④	50. ①

1. ① "내 말 무슨 뜻인지 알겠니?, 내 말 듣고 있니?" (확인)
나머지는 모두 "다시 말해주시겠어요?"

2. ④ "사실이 아니어서 유감이야."

3. ② Try one. "한 번 먹어봐."

4. ③ A : 언짢아 보이네. 왜 그리 안색이 안 좋아?
B : 야구경기에서 우승했어.

5. ① (C) 어제 빌려주었던 영화 DVD는 어땠어?

(A) 무척 좋았어. 내가 좀 더 빌려 가도 싫지 않겠니?
(D) 물론 괜찮지. 아무 때나 와.
(B) 고마워. 이번 주말에 너의 집으로 갈게.

6. ④ 그 말을 듣게 되어 유감입니다.

7. ③ 많은 책을 읽는다 - 외국어를 배운다

8. ② 나 좀 도와줄 수 있어요?

9. ④ 3일 동안 비가 내리고 있어. 곧 날씨가 개었으면 좋겠어.

10. ① have such a long face (시무룩한 표정이다) = look unhappy

11. ③ Can I try it on?
한번 입어 봐도 될까요?

12. ② 교통 혼잡

13. ② OK, I will. (알았어, 전할게.)
"가족에게 안부 전해 줘"에 대한 응답

14. ④ You can't miss it.
틀림없이 찾을 수 있을 거예요.

15. ③ A : 우리 몇 시에 만날까?
B : 피자가게에서.

16. ① Who's calling, please?
(전화) 누구세요?

17. ① A : 늦어서 미안해.
B : 천만에요.

18. ④ 도착시각은 10:30 p.m.입니다.

19. ② 아직 40분 남았어.

20. ① 미안합니다, 다른 책으로 교환해 드릴게요.

21. ② 여성 의사의 증가 추세

22. ③ 기자 - 의상 디자이너

23. ③ 동물 털 알레르기 때문에

24. ③ 채소 사 오기

25. ④ 퇴실 시간

26. ② $22

27. ① 나도 알아요. 그렇게 하지 말았어야 했는데.

28. ④ So many men, so many minds.
십인십색(十人十色)

29. ③ 작가 - 독자

30. ① M : 수업 시간에는 휴대전화를 꺼야 한다.
W : 죄송합니다. 끄는 것을 잊었어요.

31. ④ 호텔

32. ② 6:30 p.m.

33. ① 흡연 금지에 대해 언급하지 않음.

34. ④ 당신이 경주에서 이기길 바랍니다.

35. ① 원형의 모양에 산타클로스 장식이 있고 "I love you" 메시지가 담긴 케이크

36. ② a customer (고객) - a teller (은행 직원)

37. ③ 택시

38. ③ Saturday, 3 p.m. 다음날(토요일), 경기 시작 한 시간 전에 만나자고 했음.

39. ② Don't worry. You'll do a great job. 걱정하지마, 넌 매우 잘할 수 있을 거야.

40. ④ 관람객 - 미술관 직원

41. ④ A : 여보, 운전하는 동안에 주의하세요. 비가 몹시 많이 와요.
B : 알았어요. 속도를 줄일게요.

42. ① 공항

43. ④ $25
어른($10) + 어른($10) + 아이($5) = $25

44. ② 축하해! 부럽다.

45. ② 학생 – 사서
도서관에서 책을 빌리는 과정에서 일어나는 대화

46. ③ A : 안녕하세요, 머리를 어떻게 자를까요?
B : 짧게 잘라 주세요.

47. ① 사진관
여권용 사진을 찍으러 온 상황

48. ③ 가위(scissors)는 언급되지 않음
a glue stick(풀)

49. ④ 영화표 구매하기

50. ① 그렇게 해주면 고맙지.

03. 독해(단원확인문제)

1. ④	2. ③	3. ①	4. ②	5. ②
6. ④	7. ①	8. ③	9. ④	10. ②
11. ③	12. ①	13. ②	14. ④	15. ③
16. ①	17. ④	18. ③	19. ②	20. ④
21. ①	22. ①	23. ②	24. ③	25. ①
26. ④	27. ④	28. ②	29. ②	30. ③

1. ④ however
한 장소에 눈이 너무 많이 내리면, 땅과 사람 그리고 건물들에 큰 피해를 줄 수 있다. 일반적으로, 하지만, 눈은 매우 도움이 된다. 농부의 밭에 수북이 쌓인 눈은 식물이 살아 있도록 돕는다. 눈 아래에 있는 공기는 위에 있는 공기보다 훨씬 더 따듯하다.

2. ③ careful – 신중한, 주의 깊은, 조심하는
요즘 도로에는 자동차들이 점점 더 많아지고 있다. 그러나 어떤 운전자들은 자신의 운전에 주의를 기울이지 않는다.: 그들은 너무 빠르게 차를 몰던가 아니면 운전 중에 다른 생각을 한다. 결과적으로, 자동차 사고가 매우 빈번하게 발생한다. 그래서, 우리는 도로 위에서 매우 신중해야 한다.

3. ① happy
열여섯 살에, 나는 학교에 있었다. 서른두 살에, 나는 여전히 학교에 있다. 그러나 이번에는, 학생이 아니라 교사로서 학교에 있다. 내가 학생이었을 때, 내가 존경한 사람은 변호사나 의사가 아니라 선생님들이었다. 나는 학생을 가르치는 게 좋다. 학생들도 또한 나에게 배우는 것을 좋아한다.

4. ② Susan은 Tom보다 독서에 더 적은 시간을 보낸다. (Susan 2시간 / Tom 1시간)

5. ② 성격이 매우 다르다.
많은 자매처럼, Eliza와 Abby는 성격이 매우 다르다. 12살인 Eliza는 항상 뭔가 말하고 싶어 하고 공을 갖고 노는 것을 좋아한다. 반면에, 9살인 Abby는 늘 조용하며 읽을 좋은 책과 함께 있을 때 가장 행복해한다.

6. ④ urgent 긴급한
그때, 승객의 대부분은 잘 준비를 하고 있었다. 추운 바깥쪽에, 한 남자가 파도를 지켜보며 서 있었다. 갑자기, 그 앞쪽에서, 그는 물속에 있는 뭔가를 보았다. 즉시 벨을 세 번 울리며 소리를 질렀다, "빙산! 오른쪽 앞에! 멈춰!" 그러나 그때는 너무 늦었다. 그 빙산이 타이태닉호의 오른쪽 면에 300피트짜리 구멍을 만들었다. 곧, 배는 물로 가득 차고 빠르게 가라앉았다.

7. ① 수질 오염
내가 어렸을 때, 집 앞에 강이 있었다. 그 강은 매우 깨끗했었다. 나는 거기서 수영을 하고 물고기를 잡곤 했었다. 때때로 어머니는 그 강에서 빨래하곤 하셨다. 그러나, 이제 그 강은 예전만큼 깨끗하지 않다. 쓰레기로 많이 오염되었다. 그래서 나는 수영하거나 물고기를 잡으러 이제는 거기에 갈 수 없다.

8. ③
초기의 연은 다양한 목적으로 사용되었다. 한국에서, 사람들은 한 해가 끝나기 전에 악운을 날려 보내기

위해서 연을 날렸다. 연은 또한 메시지를 보내기 위해 사용되었다. (오래 전에 연은 비단과 대나무로 만들어졌다.) 때때로 사람들은 실제 전투에서 위험을 경고하기 위해 연을 사용했다. 그리고 어떤 연은 연싸움(경기)을 위해 사용되었다.

9. ④ 전쟁 중에는 자동차 부품을 만들었다.
Frank는 지금은 매우 큰 회사 사장이다. 그러나 어렸을 때 그는 작은 상점에서 일하곤 했다. 그 당시에, 그는 자전거를 고치며 하루에 열네 시간을 일했다. 여러 해 동안 돈을 모아 1938년에 자신 소유의 작은 공장을 샀다. 전쟁 동안, Frank는 비행기의 예비 부품을 만들었다. 전쟁이 끝날 무렵, 그의 작은 공장은 큰 공장이 되었다.

10. ② 실패를 두려워하지 말라.
젊을 때, 자신만의 목표를 찾으려는 시도에서 실수하는 것을 두려워할 필요가 없다. 그것은 야구나 농구 같은 운동을 배우는 것과 같다. 그 (배우는) 과정에서 꽤 많은 실수를 저지르지 않고서는 배우기를 거의 기대할 수 없다.

11. ③ clean
상어는 세상의 모든 바다에 살고 있지만, 대부분 상어는 따뜻한 물에서 산다. 때때로 상어는 병든 물고기와 병든 동물 등을 먹기 때문에, 바다가 깨끗하게 유지되도록 도움을 준다.

12. ① however
우리나라는 오랜 역사를 갖고 있다. 한국은 많은 전쟁을 겪어왔다. 과거에, 한국은 가난하고 외국에 의존했었다. 하지만, 한국은 사회적으로 그리고 경제적으로 매우 많이 발전해왔기 때문에, 이제 한국은 그 자신이 가난한 나라들을 도울 수 있다.

13. ② 연
Jane과 아빠는 무엇인가를 만드는 중이었다. 무엇을 하고 있는지 엄마에게 말씀드리지 않았다. 그들은 종이와 대나무 막대기를 사용했다. 긴 시간 동안 작업을 했다. 점심 식사 후에, Jane이 엄마에게 말씀드렸다, "우리와 공원에 가요. 엄마를 놀라게 할 만한 게 있어요." 그들 모두는 공원에 갔다. 그것은 아름다운 연이었다. 연은 하늘 높이 올라갔다.

14. ④ 문화에 따라 선호하는 음식이 다르다.
당신은 무슨 종류의 음식을 먹고 싶어 하는가? 많은 사람이 그들 자신의 문화에서 나온 음식을 먹는 것을 선호한다. 어떤 사람들은 특정한 음식이 익숙하지 않기에 싫어한다. 일본인들은 생 말고기를 즐겨 먹지만, 그것을 맛보고 싶어 하는 미국인은 거의 없을 것이다. 많은 아시아인은 미국에서 매우 인기 있는 음식인 피자를 좋아하지 않는다.

15. ③
집을 떠나기 전에 비행기에서 무엇을 입을지 신중하게 생각해 보라. 꽉 끼지 않는 편안한 옷을 골라라. 비행 중에 발이 커지므로 편한 신발을 신어라. 신발이 꽉 끼면 불편할 것이다. (당신이 읽을 수 있는 책을 골라라.) 비행기에서 신을 수 있는 슬리퍼를 가져갈 수 있다.

16. ① 컴퓨터 마우스의 유래
컴퓨터 마우스는 1964년에 발명되었다. 최초의 마우스는 나무로 만들어졌고, 딱 하나의 버튼만 있었다. 컴퓨터 마우스는 1984년에 처음으로 사용되었다. 오늘날에는 거의 모든 컴퓨터에 마우스가 있다. 당신은 컴퓨터의 기본화면에서 커서를 움직이기 위해 마우스를 사용한다. 비록 마우스가 1964년에 발명되었지만, 대중적으로 사용하기까지 약 20년이 걸렸다.

17. ④ 영어를 쉽게 배우는 방법
어떤 사람들은 새로운 언어를 쉽게 배운다. 다른 사람들은 새로운 언어를 배우는 데 어려움을 겪는다. 영어와 같은 외국어를 당신 혼자 배우는 것을 어떻게 도울 수 있을까? 영어 학습을 좀 더 쉽고 좀 더 재미있게 만들어 주는 몇 가지 방법이 있다.

18. ③ 피라미드
그것들은 이집트의 왕이나 여왕을 위한 무덤으로 지어졌다. 그것들은 거대한 돌로 만들어졌다. 대개, 죽은 파라오(이집트의 왕)가 보관되는 방이 하나 있다. 이집트 사람들은 사후의 세계(내세)가 있다고 믿었다. 그것들은 왕들이 다른 삶으로의 여정에 필요한 모든 것을 제공하도록 설계되었다.

19. ② 공공장소에서 남을 배려하자.
지난 일요일, 햇빛을 즐기러 집 근처의 공원에 갔었다. 매우 시끄럽게 떠드는 사람이 많았다. 몇몇 젊은 이들은 음악을 크게 틀어놓고 춤을 추었다. 크게 짖는 개도 있었으나 개 주인은 내버려 두었다. 공원이 너무 시끄러워서 나는 쉬지를 못했다. 내 생각에는, 공공장소에서는 다른 사람들을 배려해야 한다고 생각한다.

20. ④
인간이 존재하기 오래 전부터 자연은 존재했다. 최초의 인간은 자연스러운 방식으로 살았다. 그들은 먹을 수 있는 과일, 열매 그리고 뿌리 등을 모았다. 그들은 돌을 잘라 도구로 만들지 못했다. 그들은 자연을 바꾸지 못했다. (나중에 인간들은 자연을 통제하는 법을 배우기 시작했다.) 그들은 식량을 재배하기 위한 도구를 만들었고, 동물을 사냥하기 위한 무기를 만들었다.

21. ① 뜻이 있는 곳에 길이 있다.
구두 광택제로 손이 시커멓게 된 소년이 있었다. 그러나 그의 두 눈은 희망으로 빛났다. 무척 어려울 때조차도 소년은 미소를 지으려고 애썼다. 사람들은 소년에게 구두 닦는 것을 좋아하는지 물었다. 그는 대답했다, "물론이지요, 나는 희망을 닦고 있는 거랍니다." 후에, 이 소년은 '모던타임즈와 더 키드'를 만든 찰리 채플린이라는 훌륭한 영화배우이자 제작자가 되었다.

22. ① come true – 실현되다
꿈을 갖는 것은 항상 매우 좋다. 그러나 당신의 꿈을 성취하기 위해서는 열심히 노력해야 한다. 댄서가 되기 위해서, 매일 춤 연습하는 것을 규칙으로 삼아라. 로마는 하루아침에 이루어진 것이 아니다.

↓

열심히 노력해라, 그러면 당신의 꿈은 실현될 것이다.

23. ② symbols – 상징
사람, 장소, 물건 또는 사건은 그것 자체의 의미를 지니고 있으며, 또한 그 자체 너머의 어떤 것을 상징한다. 상징의 예는 음악, 텔레비전, 그리고 일상의 대화 등 우리 주변의 어디에나 존재한다. 비둘기는 평화를 나타내고, 빨간 장미는 진정한 사랑을 상징한다.

24. ③ make errors – 실수를 저지르다
인간의 기억은 비디오카메라처럼 작동하지 않는다. 기억은 실제로 여러 면에서 약하다. 기억과정의 모든 단계에서, 사람들이 실수를 저지르는 게 가능하다. 예를 들어, 매년 미국에서 약 4천 명의 사람들이 잘못된 목격자 때문에 체포된다. 그들은 눈으로 보지 못한 사람이나 사건을 만들어낼지도 모른다.

25. ① 식용 가능한 식물을 찾아서 재배해야 한다.
세계인구가 증가함에 따라, (세계의 여러) 나라들은 더 많은 식량을 생산해야 한다. 어떻게 이 문제를 해결할 수 있을까? 식량 공급을 늘리는 하나의 방법은 사람들이 다양한 종류의 식물을 먹기 시작하는 것이다. 사람이 먹을 수 있는 식물의 종류는 2만 가지가 있다. 그러므로 우리는 그 식물 중 일부를 재배하고 먹을 방법을 찾아야 한다.

26. ④ 의사로서 전쟁에 자원했다.
어니스트 헤밍웨이는 일리노이주, 오크 파크에서 태어났다. 그러나 그는 미시간주 북부에서 17년을 보냈는데, 그곳에서 그의 아버지가 그에게 사냥과 낚시를 알려 주었다. 고등학교에 다닐 때, 헤밍웨이는 권투와 미식축구를 했다. 미국이 제1차 세계대전에 참전했을 때 그는 자원하여 이탈리아에서 미국의 구급차 운전사가 되었다. 전쟁에서 돌아온 후 그는 많은 전쟁 관련 소설들을 썼다.

27. ④ (C)–(B)–(A)
일본인은 세상에서 가장 건강한 사람 중의 하나라고 여겨진다.
(C) 예를 들어, 그들의 심장병과 암 발생률은 다른 나라의 발생률보다 훨씬 더 낮다.
(B) 일본인이 그런 장점을 누릴 수 있는 이유를 찾으려고 많은 의사가 노력해 왔다.
(A) 이 의사들에 따르면 가장 중요한 요소가 세 가지 있는데, 그것은 식습관, 운동, 생활양식이다.

28. ② avoid – 피하다
이메일은 정보화 시대에 있어서 기본적인 통신수단이 되어 왔다. 하지만, 이메일은 사람들이 스팸메일을 차단함에 따라 곧 쓸모없게 될 수도 있다. 긴 이메일 이름을 선택하는 것은 스팸메일을 받는 것을 막는 좋은 방법이다. 문자와 숫자를 섞어서 사용하라. 이것은 스팸메일 프로그램이 당신의 이메일을 찾을 가능성을 감소시킨다.

↓

긴 이메일 이름을 사용하는 것은 스팸메일을 받는 것을 피하는 좋은 방법이다.

29. ② 다섯 개의 눈이 크기가 같다.
꿀벌은 모든 곤충과 마찬가지로 세 부분으로 나뉜 몸을 가지고 있다. 꿀벌은 다섯 개의 눈을 갖고 있다: 머리 위에 삼각형을 이루는 작은 눈 세 개와 머리 양쪽에 있는 큰 눈이다. 벌은 가슴 양쪽에 각각 세 개의 다리가 있다. 꿀벌은 걷거나 몸에서 꽃가루를 털어내기 위해 다리를 사용한다. 벌은 물과 꿀을 마시기 위해 혀를 사용한다.

30. ③ However - 하지만
줄무늬는 어떻게 얼룩말을 보호할까? 여러분은 아프리카에서 흑백 얼룩말이 무리들 사이에서 두드러져 지나가는 사자의 쉬운 표적이 된다고 생각할지도 모른다. 하지만, 얼룩말의 줄무늬는 실제로 그 동물들이 야외에 숨는 것을 돕는다. 멀리서 보면 얼룩말 무리가 마치 흑백의 물결처럼 보이게 되어 배고픈 사자를 혼란스럽게 한다. 사자는 공격할 동물을 한 마리도 골라내지 못한다. 사자는 멀리 사라지고, 얼룩말은 목숨을 건진다.

실전모의고사

01. 실전모의고사

1. ②	2. ④	3. ①	4. ③	5. ④
6. ②	7. ③	8. ①	9. ③	10. ②
11. ④	12. ①	13. ①	14. ②	15. ③
16. ④	17. ③	18. ②	19. ①	20. ④
21. ②	22. ④	23. ④	24. ①	25. ③

1. ② 노력
너는 너의 일(공부)에 더 큰 노력을 해야 한다.

2. ④ remember 기억하다
keep in mind : ~을 명심하다, 기억하다
제발, 내가 말했던 것을 명심해라.

3. ① 부끄럽다
나는 내가 너무 많은 실수를 해서 부끄럽다.

4. ③ 동의어 (게으른) / 나머지는 반의어
① 넓은 - 좁은 ② 깊은 - 얕은
④ 높은 - 낮은

5. ④ 아이의 손이 닿지 않는 곳에 보관한다.

6. ② patient (형용사) 인내심 있는 / (명사) 환자
· 마지막으로, 너는 인내심이 있어야 한다.
· 그 환자는 오늘 훨씬 더 좋아졌다.

7. ③ store (명사) 상점, 가게 / (동사) 저장하다
· 길 맞은편에 식료품 가게가 있다.
· 그들은 비행기에 동력을 공급하기 위해 태양 빛을 저장한다.

8. ① if (접속사) 만약 ~라면 / ~인지 아닌지
· 네가 원한다면, 콘서트에 가도 좋아.
· 그는 나에게 중국어를 아는지 모르는지 물었다.

9. ③ 겉만 보고 속을 판단하지 마라.
A : 엄마는 "책의 표지로 책을 판단하지 마라"라고 자주 말씀하신다.
B : 그게 무슨 뜻이니?

10. ② worried 걱정되는
A : 면접은 잘 보았니?
B : 잘 모르겠어. 결과가 오늘 나오는데.
A : 정말? 오늘 좋은 소식이 있을 거라고 생각해.
B : 그렇게 생각하니? 걱정이 멈추질 않아.
A : 걱정하지 마. 너는 그 일에 딱 맞는 사람이야.

11. ④ a lost & found office 분실물 보관소
A : 어떻게 도와드릴까요?
B : 지갑을 잃어버렸습니다. 누가 돌려주었는지 확인하러 왔습니다.
A : 지갑이 어떻게 생겼는지요?
B : 빨간색이고요, 옆에 지퍼가 있습니다.
A : 빨간 지갑이요? 오, 이게 당신 것인가요?

12. ① I'd love to, but I can't.
A : 나와 함께 갈 수 있니?
B : 그러고 싶지만, 할 수 없어요. 해야 할 일이 많아요.

13. ① I'm sorry I don't have a watch.
A : 몇 시인가요?
B : 미안하지만, 시계가 없습니다.

14. ② (B) - (A) - (C)
가방에 짐 싸는 것은 끝냈니?
(B) 거의 다 쌌어요.
(A) 좋아. 일찍 자는 게 좋겠구나.
(C) 네, 엄마. 7시에 깨워 주시겠어요?

15. ③ B
Karl Landsteiner는 1900년에 처음으로 혈액형에 이름 붙이는 것을 생각해냈다. 그는 혈액을 A, B, AB, O와 같이 4가지로 분류했다. O형은 세상에서 가장 흔한 혈액형이다. A형은 두 번째로 흔하며, AB형은 가장 드문 혈액형이다.

16. ④ 불평
나는 공항 근처에 산다. 제트기가 밤낮으로 우리 집 위로 날아다닌다. 제트기는 내 사생활을 침해한다. 책을 읽을 수 없고 TV도 볼 수 없다. 우리 옆집에 노인이 한 분 사신다. 그도 소음으로 고통을 겪는다. 그는 아파서 지금 병원에 입원해 있다.

17. ③ spam
버튼을 한 번 클릭함으로써 수백만 명의 이메일 사용자에게 이것이 보내질 수 있다. 때때로 이것은 많은 컴퓨터에 해로운 바이러스를 퍼뜨린다.

18. ②
우리의 귀를 보호하기 위해 우리가 할 수 있는 것이 몇 가지 있다. 큰 소리는 귀에 해로울 수 있다. 이 때문에 우리는 다른 사람의 귀에 소리를 질러서는 안 된다. 귀를 때리는 것도 해로울 수 있다. 그래서 다른 이의 귀를 절대로 때리지 마라. 귀에 뭔가를 집어넣는 것도 조심하라.

19. ① 아프리카 기아의 원인
아프리카의 기아에는 많은 원인이 있다. 아프리카의 정부들은 급속한 인구 증가 때문에, 모든 국민에게 충분한 식량을 공급할 수 없다. 두 번째로, 오랜 기간 비가 오지 않아 종종 사람들이 먹을 것이 거의 없다. 또한, 많은 내전과 열악한 운송수단이 기아의 원인이 된다.

20. ④ memory
많은 사람이 기억 상실에 대해 걱정하지만, 전문가들은 뭔가를 잊는다는 것이 정상적이라고 말한다. 만약 우리가 모든 것을 기억한다면, 우리는 많은 어려움을 겪게 될 것이다. 잊는다는 것은 기억만큼 중요하다.

21. ② at home
집에서 영화를 보는 것은 매우 편리하며, 비용이 훨씬 적게 든다. 사람들은 간식을 만들기 위해 영화를 멈출 수 있고, 전화를 받을 수 있으며, 아기를 확인할 수 있다. 서 있어야 할 긴 줄이 없고 사야 할 표도 없다.

22. ④ 평균 수명이 25년이다.
초콜릿은 카카오나무에서 나온다. 이 나무들은 덥고 습한 열대 기후를 가진 나라에서 잘 자란다. 그들은 6m 정도의 높이에 커다란 초록 잎사귀들을 가지고 있다. 초콜릿은 그 나무의 열매인 카카오 열매로 만들어진다. 카카오나무는 3~4살 때 첫 번째 열매를 가진다. 몇몇 카카오나무들은 200살까지 자라지만, 대부분 나무는 약 25년 동안 열매를 맺는다.

23. ④
물은 태양이 그 위에 빛나고 있을 때 따뜻하다. 이 물의 일부는 하늘로 올라가 구름이 된다. 바람은 그 구름을 수백 킬로미터나 나른다. 그러면 구름은 하늘의 차가운 공기를 만나고 우리는 물방울을 본다. (그래서 물은 늘 강에서 바다로 흘러가는 것이다.) 그 물방울들이 비이다.

[24~25]
우리는 규칙적인 운동이 우리 몸에 좋다는 것을 안다. 그러나 우리 대부분은 운동 전에 약간의 스트레칭을 해야 한다는 것을 알지 못한다. 스트레칭에서 얻을 수 있는 많은 이점이 있다. 스트레칭은 몸이 더 유연해지도록 하고 몸이 균형을 유지하는 데 도움을 준다. 더욱이, 그것은 몸매를 유지해주고, 근육이 다치는 것을 예방한다. 그것은 또한 스트레스를 줄여줄 수 있다.

24. ① In addition

25. ③ 스트레칭의 좋은 점

02. 실전모의고사

1. ③	2. ①	3. ②	4. ④	5. ③
6. ②	7. ①	8. ④	9. ③	10. ④
11. ②	12. ①	13. ④	14. ③	15. ②
16. ①	17. ①	18. ②	19. ③	20. ④
21. ②	22. ③	23. ③	24. ④	25. ①

1. ③ 만족한
be satisfied with ~에 만족하다
그는 그 결과에 만족했다.

2. ① 이해하다
make out 이해하다 = understand
나는 그녀가 말했던 것을 이해할 수 없었다.

3. ② happened
take place 발생하다 = happen, occur
교통사고가 버스 정거장 근처에서 발생했다.

4. ④ grow (동사) 자라다 – growth (명사) 성장
나머지는 형용사 – 명사의 관계

5. ③ called
목적어인 my name과 목적 보어인 called의 관계는 수동이므로 과거분사를 쓴다.
나는 내 뒤에서 내 이름이 불리는 걸 들었다.

6. ② how much it is
간접의문문 : 의문사 + 주어 + 동사
너는 그것의 가격이 얼마인지 아니?

7. ① others
여러 사람 중에서 어떤 사람은(some) ~, 다른 사람은(others) …
여름에, 어떤 사람들은 바닷가로 가고, 다른 이들은 산으로 간다.

8. ④ He does his homework. – 그는 숙제한다.
A : What does he do for a living?
– 그는 직업이 무엇이니?

9. ③ passenger 승객 – taxi driver 택시 기사
A : 동대문 운동장까지 가주세요.
B : 네. 경기를 보러 가시나요, 부인?
A : 아니오. 쇼핑하러 갑니다.
B : 아, 알겠어요. 안전벨트를 매 주세요.

10. ④ In a shoe store (신발가게)
A : 도움이 필요하세요?
B : 네. 부츠 한 켤레 찾고 있어요.
A : 미안합니다. 부츠가 없는데요. 샌들은 어떤가요?
B : 샌들이요? 좋지요. 파란색 샌들이 있나요?

11. ② 격려
A : 있잖아, 과학시험에서 F를 받았어.
B : 유감이네. 하지만 힘내라! 나는 네가 다음 번에 더 잘할 거라 확신해.

12. ① Money (돈)
나는 모든 나라에서 발견된다. 사람들은 쇼핑하러 갈 때, 나를 가지고 다닌다. 대부분 사람은 나를 얻기 위해 일을 해야만 한다. (물건을) 사고, 파는 일은 나와 함께 이루어진다. 나는 구리, 은 그리고 종이로 만들어진다.

13. ④ Weight (체중)
체중 조절은 당신의 건강에 중요하다. 만약 당신이 살이 찐다면, 당신은 심장마비를 일으킬 수도 있다. 그러므로 당신은 체중을 조절해야만 한다.

14. ③ kind
Mr. Pott는 어려움에 부딪힌 것은 누구든, 어느 것이든 도와줄 것이다. 그것은 날개가 부러진 새일 수도 있다. Mr. Pott는 그 새가 건강해지도록 무엇을 해야 할지 알 것이다. 그는 그 새를 돌보고, 먹이를 가져다주고, 날개가 치료될 때까지 지켜볼 것이다.

15. ② talk
어머니나 아버지는 종종 한 아이의 첫 번째 읽기 선생님이 된다. 아기에게 말을 함으로써, 부모들은 아기가 언어란 무엇이며, 언어가 왜 필요한지 이해하는 것을 돕는다. 아이들은 말소리에서 사랑을 느낀다. 그들은 말대꾸(talk back)하려고 애쓴다. 아기들은 듣고 말하면서, 사실과 생각들을 저장한다.

16. ① deserts (사막)
모래는 전 세계에서 발견된다. 어떤 모래는 바로 우리 주변의 땅에 있다. 모래 대부분은 바다와 호수의 바닥에 있다. 모래는 강바닥을 따라 굴러다니며 때로는 강둑(river bank)까지 퍼져 나간다. 대부분 사막은 모래로 덮여 있는 건조한 장소이다.

17. ① insect (곤충)
그들은 척추가 없는 동물이다. 수백만 종의 다른 종

류들이 존재한다. 그들은 머리, 가운데 부분, 뒷부분의 세 부분으로 나누어진다. 그들은 모두 한 쌍의 더듬이(feeler)를 지니고 있으며, 여섯 개의 다리를 갖고 있다.

18. ② (C) – (A) – (B)
당신의 손을 보라. 당신이 손을 보기 위해서는 많은 일이 일어나야만 한다. 먼저 손의 영상이 당신의 눈에 만들어진다.
(C) 그러면, 그 영상에 대한 메시지가 눈에서 당신의 뇌로 전달된다.
(A) 이 메시지는 당신이 그 영상에 대해 생각하게 한다.
(B) 이 모든 일이 일어난 후에 당신은 손을 보게 된다.

19. ③ 바닷물이 짠 이유
빗물은 움직이면서, 땅과 바위에서 소금을 흡수한다. 이 물이 소금기를 강으로 가져간다. 소금기가 있는 강물은 바다로 흘러 들어간다. 강물은 아주 오랜 시간 동안 바다로 흘러 들어가고 있다. 그래서 바다에는 소금이 많다.

20. ④ 매일 이용할 수 있다.
금요일에서 일요일까지 운행함

21. ② to advise – 충고하기 위해서
영어를 실제로 자주 사용하면 할수록, 당신은 더욱 빠르게 배우게 된다. 실수하는 것을 두려워하지 않고 끊임없이 말하기와 쓰기를 계속하는 것은 유용하다.

22. ③ 좋은 공부 습관을 위한 비결
당신은 어떤 종류의 공부 습관을 갖고 있는가? 당신의 공부 습관이 효과적이라고 생각하는가? 좋은 공부 습관은 시간과 노력을 덜어줄 수 있다. 좋은 공부 습관을 개발하는 데 도움이 되는 몇 가지 비결(tip)이 여기 있다.

23. ③ They were very expensive for them.
여기에 오늘날 많은 사람이 입는 것을 만든 한 남자의 이야기가 있다. 그의 이름은 Levi Strauss이다. 그는 19세기에 미국에서 청바지를 만들어 팔기 시작했다. 청바지는 노동자를 위한 안성맞춤의 옷이기 때문에 잘 팔렸다. (③ 그것은 노동자에게는 매우 비쌌다.) 젊은 사람들도 청바지를 매우 좋아했다. 젊은 이들에게 있어, 청바지를 입는 것은 반항의 한 형태였다.

[24~25]
옛날에 전투에서 패배한 왕이 있었다. 그가 적으로부터 피해 동굴에 은신하고 있을 때, 그는 거미를 보았다. 그것은 거미집을 만들려고 하고 있었다. 위로 올라가자 거미집 속의 거미줄이 끊어져 아래로 떨어졌다. 그러나 그것은 포기하지 않았다. 거미는 계속해서 오르려고 시도했다. 마침내 거미는 성공적으로 거미집을 완성했다. 왕은 생각했다, "작은 거미가 그렇게 용감하게 실패를 마주할 수 있다면, 왜 내가 포기해야 할까?" 그리고는 군사를 모아 적과 거듭 싸웠다. 마침내 그는 왕국을 되찾았다.

24. ④ occasionally 때때로
나머지는 모두 결국, 마침내

25. ① 포기하지 않고 계속 도전해야 한다.

영어

인쇄일		2022년 4월 27일
발행일		2022년 5월 4일
펴낸이		(주)매경아이씨
펴낸곳		도서출판 **국자감**
지은이		편집부
주소		서울시 영등포구 문래2가 32번지
전화		1544-4696
등록번호		2008.03.25 제 300-2008-28호
ISBN		979-11-5518-129-4 13370

국자감 전문서적

기초다지기 / 기초굳히기

"기초다지기, 기초굳히기 한권으로 시작하는 검정고시 첫걸음"

· 기초부터 차근차근 시작할 수 있는 교재
· 기초가 없어 시작을 망설이는 수험생을 위한 교재

기본서

**"단기간에 합격! 효율적인 학습!
적중률 100%에 도전!"**

· 철저하고 꼼꼼한 교육과정 분석에서 나온 탄탄한 구성
· 한눈에 쏙쏙 들어오는 내용정리
· 최고의 강사진으로 구성된 동영상 강의

만점 전략서

"검정고시 합격은 기본! 고득점과 대학진학은 필수!"

· 검정고시 고득점을 위한 유형별 요약부터
문제풀이까지 한번에
· 기본 다지기부터 단원 확인까지 실력점검

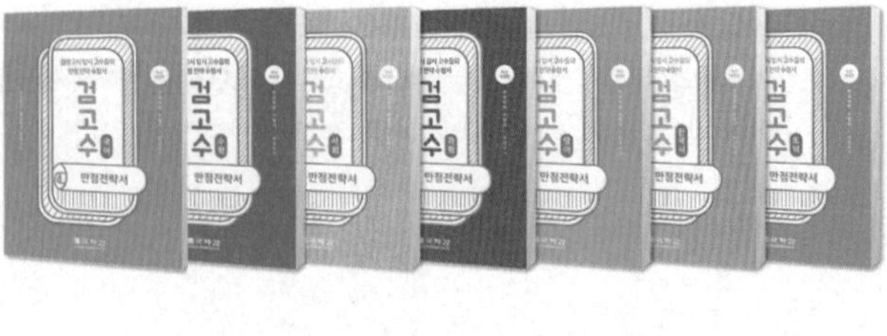

www.kukjagam.co.kr

핵심 총정리

"시험 전 총정리가 필요한 이 시점! 모든 내용이 한눈에"

· 단 한권에 담아낸 완벽학습 솔루션
· 출제경향을 반영한 핵심요약정리

합격길라잡이

"개념 4주 다이어트, 교재도 다이어트한다!"

· 요점만 정리되어 있는 교재로 단기간 시험범위 완전정복!
· 합격길라잡이 한권이면 합격은 기본!

기출문제집

"시험장에 있는 이 기분! 기출문제로 시험문제 유형 파악하기"

· 기출을 보면 답이 보인다
· 차원이 다른 상세한 기출문제풀이 해설

예상문제

"오랜기간 노하우로 만들어낸 신들린 입시고수들의 예상문제"

· 출제 경향과 빈도를 분석한 예상문제와 정확한 해설
· 시험에 나올 문제만 예상해서 풀이한다

한양 프로그램 한눈에 보기

· 검정고시반 중·고졸 검정고시 수업으로 한번에 합격!

기초개념	기본이론	핵심정리	핵심요약	파이널
개념 익히기	과목별 기본서로 기본 다지기	핵심 총정리로 출제 유형 분석 경향 파악	요약정리 중요내용 체크	실전 모의고사 예상문제 기출문제 완성

· 고득점관리반 검정고시 합격은 기본 고득점은 필수!

기초개념	기본이론	심화이론	핵심정리	핵심요약	파이널
전범위 개념익히기	과목별 기본서로 기본 다지기	만점 전략서로 만점대비	핵심 총정리로 출제 유형 분석 경향 파악	요약정리 중요내용 체크 오류범위 보완	실전 모의고사 예상문제 기출문제 완성

· 대학진학반 고졸과 대학입시를 한번에!

기초학습	기본학습	심화학습/검정고시 대비	핵심요약	문제풀이, 총정리
기초학습과정 습득 학생별 인강 부교재 설정	진단평가 및 개별학습 피드백 수업방향 및 난이도 조절 상담	모의평가 결과 진단 및 상담 4월 검정고시 대비 집중수업	자기주도 과정 및 부교재 재설정 4월 검정고시 성적에 따른 재시험 및 수시컨설팅 준비	전형별 입시진행 연계교재 완성도 평가

· 수능집중반 정시준비도 전략적으로 준비한다!

기초학습	기본학습	심화학습	핵심요약	문제풀이, 총정리
기초학습과정 습득 학생별 인강 부교재 설정	진단평가 및 개별학습 피드백 수업방향 및 난이도 조절 상담	모의고사 결과진단 및 상담 / EBS 연계 교재 설정 / 학생별 학습성취 사항 평가	자기주도 과정 및 부교재 재설정 학생별 개별지도 방향 점검	전형별 입시진행 연계교재 완성도 평가

D-DAY를 위한 신의 한수
검정고시생 대학진학 입시 전문
검정고시 합격은 기본!
대학진학은 필수!
입시 전문가의 컨설팅으로 성적을 뛰어넘는 결과를 만나보세요!
HANYANG ACADEMY
YouTube
HANYANG
ACADEMY

모든 수험생이 꿈꾸는 더 완벽한 입시 준비!

입시전략 컨설팅 · 수시전략 컨설팅 · 자기소개서 컨설팅

면접 컨설팅 · 논술 컨설팅 · 정시전략 컨설팅

입시전략 컨설팅

학생 현재 상태를 파악하고 희망 대학 합격 가능성을 진단해 목표를 달성 할 수 있도록 3중 케어

수시전략 컨설팅

학생 성적에 꼭 맞는 대학 선정으로 합격률 상승! 검정고시 (혹은 모의고사) 성적에 따른 전략적인 지원으로 현실성 있는 최상의 결과 보장

자기소개서 컨설팅

지원동기부터 학과 적합성까지 한번에! 학생만의 스토리를 녹여 강점은 극대화 하고 단점은 보완하는 밀착 첨삭 자기소개서

면접 컨설팅

기초인성면접부터 대학별 기출예상질문 대비와 모의촬영으로 실전면접 완벽하게 대비

대학별 고사 (논술)

최근 5개년 기출문제 분석 및 빈출 주제를 정리하여 인문 논술의 트렌드를 강의! 지문의 정확한 이해와 글의 요약부터 밀착형 첨삭까지 한번에!

정시전략 컨설팅

빅데이터와 전문 컨설턴트의 노하우 / 실제 합격 사례 기반 전문 컨설팅

HANYANG
ACADEMY